Dugout Wisdom

LIFE LESSONS FROM BASEBALL

CAPTURED BY DAN MIGALA

Dugout Wisdom:
Life Lessons from Baseball

By Dan Migala

ISBN: 978-0-6152-1396-5

D E D I C A T I O N_____.

Dugout Wisdom is a reflection of a lifetime love with baseball and Roland Hemond and is dedicated to honoring the memory of Bill Davis. Bill, you're the best friend I've ever known. Thank you for continually showing me the rainbows that are always in our presence.

P R E F A C E————————————————————•

"Dreams are really about pursuing a feeling." • Rod Carew

I can't help but think that Rod's words are a perfect explanation for why I wrote this book.

Writing *Dugout Wisdom* had not been a long-held dream of mine, but as I continued working on it, I felt more and more like I was born to do it. Rod said that when he was on the baseball field, he felt at peace and wanted to pursue that feeling as much as he could. Having completed *Dugout Wisdom*, I know exactly what he meant.

And it is that feeling that I hope this book inspires through its tales of destiny, fate, and dreams.

Like everyone featured in these pages, as a child I vividly dreamed of hearing my name echo over a major league stadium public address system as I stepped confidently into the batter's box.

As it turned out, fate had other plans for me.

While I will never know what it feels like to face a big-league curveball or hear the roar of the crowd as I circle the bases, I am now, thanks to the heartfelt conversations captured in this book, a more emotionally intelligent man. I have a newfound understanding of the passion it takes to have courage, discipline, and sacrifice in order to achieve your dream.

I also learned that there are more similarities than I realized between everyday people like you and me and the greatest of baseball players.

Through George Brett's thoughts about struggling through his first major league season, I learned about humility.

From my mutually vulnerable conversation with Kirby Puckett—just a day before he passed away—I learned about removing fear of failure and replacing it with unconditional faith.

By speaking with Ryne Sandberg, who was my favorite baseball player when I was growing up outside of Chicago, I learned the need to step outside of my comfort zone to better myself.

And by listening to Sparky Anderson, I learned to follow the signs that manifest themselves in our everyday encounters. Sparky said his entire life was changed because he simply followed a sign—a baseball, of course—that found its way into his life:

"I believe so strongly that there are only a handful of people you will encounter in life that will completely change your destiny. You have to be open to following the baseballs in your life and letting these people come into your life every day because you might miss them."

I discovered one of my baseballs, one of my destiny changers, in Duke Snider, the first person I interviewed for this book. I was extremely nervous about talking to Duke, but when the interview began, I felt like I was listening to one of my grandfather's tales, and my nerves were quickly settled.

Duke shared a wonderful story about his first spring training. After the interview, he told me he was surprised that he had opened up to me in a way he had not done before with a journalist. When I asked him why he felt this way, he said: "You never asked me what I thought about my destiny-changing moment. You asked me what I *felt*."

Duke suggested that, for all of my interviews still to come, I should ask players to focus on their *feelings* rather than their *thoughts*. "I know you will get the other players to open up their emotions," he told me. "I know I did in a way I never have before."

Duke's advice impacted me in so many more ways than simply how to approach the remaining interviews. I gained a much deeper understanding of how to connect with people and a new way to appreciate the difficult-to-grasp human emotion of passion.

I'll forever keep a special place in my heart for the men and women in this book who shared their memories, their feelings, and their personal interpretation of passion. Thanks to each of them, I will forever believe that passion is the precise blending of what your heart feels and your mind knows to be true.

• Dan Migala

F O R E W O R D_____•

Baseball is covered like no other sport. As such, we all seem to know everything about every player during his or her career. But far too often, we forget—or don't know—what's truly been important, inspirational, and motivational, allowing those fortunate enough to have been involved in the game and to succeed.

It takes a special person to be a major league athlete, and for many of our heroes, there's a story that helps explain what drives them. Some of them are shared here.

As a longtime baseball executive, I know many of these stories and have one of my own.

In 1951, I had taken a leave from the United States Coast Guard and dreamed of getting a job in baseball. I traveled by plane and even hitchhiked a little to arrive in DeLand, Florida, the spring training home of the Pittsburgh Pirates for whom my cousin, Ray Lague, was a pitcher in their farm system.

Ray had not arrived to camp, but I met a very friendly woman named Mrs. Katherine McMahon. I talked with her for a few minutes and asked her, since Ray was not there, if she could drive me into town so I could take the bus to St. Petersburg to see more spring training games.

We began talking, and she introduced me to her husband, Sergeant Leo McMahon. He was a professional baseball player prior to enlisting in the military at the onset of World War I. Sadly, he was the victim of a mustard gas injury that instantly took away his sight, but not his spirit. This conversation continued, and the McMahons invited me to stay at their home over the weekend.

Trusting my gut, I took them up on the opportunity.

I was instantly drawn to them and fascinated with their stories about life and baseball. The McMahons spent their summers touring minor league baseball towns. Sergeant McMahon would dress in his Army uniform and sing the national anthem under the billing of the "Lucky Sergeant." They supported themselves simply by passing around a cap in the crowd and asking fans to make donations.

Stories like this struck a chord in me and further ignited the love of baseball that was in my belly. I think he realized also how much I loved baseball and suggested I correspond with two of his favorite baseball men: Fresco Thompson, farm director of the Brooklyn Dodgers, and Charlie Blossfield, general manager of the Hartford's minor league team.

Sergeant McMahon dictated letters of introduction to Messrs. Thompson and Blossfield. I quickly followed up these letters by visiting these two gentlemen. Mr. Thompson was very cordial, but the Dodgers had no openings. Mr. Blossfield, however, did have an opening. On July 3, 1951, I started my job with the Hartford Chiefs in a role that would be considered an intern today.

Serendipitously, the night on which I was hired was when J. A. "Bob" Quinn was honored at Morgan G. Buckley Stadium in Hartford. Little did I know at the time that a young girl at the ceremony, Bob Quinn's granddaughter, Margo Quinn, would become my wife on November 8, 1958.

This may appear to be a storybook development. Well, it was, and it is. And, as you will see throughout the pages of this book, it is just the beginning of the tales of destiny, dreams, and fate that are the foundation of everyone who has achieved greatness in this game—on or off the field.

• Roland Hemond

T R I B U T E

Before reading this book, we should give special thanks to all of those who so graciously agreed to be interviewed in sharing their destiny-altering moments. Each person was especially pleased in knowing that the National Baseball Hall of Fame, the Professional Baseball Scouts Foundation (PBSF), and the Association of Professional Ball Players of America (APBPA) benefit from sales of this book.

As a fitting and subtle tribute to each scout, the players were asked to name the scouts responsible for initially signing them.

For your reference, their names are listed after the corresponding profiles.

For the scouts themselves and their friends and families reading, please take tremendous comfort that every player smiled brightly and spoke lovingly when asked about their scout—serving as a fitting tribute to these unsung heroes of baseball.

STARTING LINEUP_____•

- Manager: Cincinnati Reds 1970–1978, Detroit Tigers 1979–1995
- American League Manager of the Year: 1984, 1987
- Elected to the National Baseball Hall of Fame: 2000

SPARKY ANDERSON———.

There are only a handful of people you will encounter in life
that will completely change your destiny.

In 1942, I was nine years old, and my family had just moved from South Dakota to California. We moved into a house that was tucked just beyond the right field fence of the University of Southern California baseball field.

One day, I came home from school and found a baseball in the bushes that had come over the fence of the baseball field. I picked up the baseball and walked over to the field and asked one of the players, "Who is the boss around here?"

They pointed to the team's manager, and that was when I met Rod Dadeux for the first time.

I asked him, "Are you the boss?"

He smiled and nodded yes.

I returned the baseball to him, and he said, "You are an honest young man. Would you like to be my batboy?"

I did not know anything about baseball at this time in my life, and I definitely did not know what a batboy was, but I still said yes.

Rod told me I could do it under two conditions. The rules were I needed to get my parent's permission, and I had to show him my report card every time I had one.

He took me in like I was his son, and he did so much for me during that time. He helped me to develop a love of baseball and a love of life. I watched him intensely and saw how he appreciated all the gifts God gave him.

He showed me the importance of being fortunate and never thinking you are better than anyone.

Rod used to tell me, "When you are fortunate, it is a tremendous gift. It is impossible to be better than someone, but you can be more fortunate."

He taught me how to cradle this attitude in everything you do, and I did every day of my life.

To this day, meeting him was the greatest thing that ever happened to me in my professional life. It was even greater than winning the World Series as the manager of the Cincinnati Reds and the Detroit Tigers.

You see, I strongly believe that there are only a handful of people you will encounter in life that will completely change your destiny. You have to be open to following the baseballs in your life and letting these people come into your life every day because you might miss them.

And how fortunate am I that I met my destiny changer when I was only nine years old?

Fortunate indeed.

Scout: Harold "Lefty" Phillips

- Wins 287 • ERA 3.31 • Strikeouts 3,701
- Minnesota Twins 1970–1976, 1985–1988, Texas Rangers 1976–1977, Pittsburgh Pirates 1978–1980, Cleveland Indians 1981–1985, California Angels 1989–1992
- American League Western Division Champion: 1970, 1987
- All-Star: 1973, 1985
- National League Eastern Division Champion: 1979
- World Series Champion: 1979, 1987

BERT BLYLEVEN———•

Life is just too short to fail.

In 1979, I spent my first season in the National League with the Pittsburgh Pirates and was on my first World Series champion team.

It should have been one of my career high points, but it wasn't.

I finished the season with a 12-5 won-loss record and 20 no-decisions—that was a major league record at the time for no-decisions. I was so frustrated that even though the team won 31 of my 37 starts, I did not have the personal record to show for it. I was also upset because our team was loaded with superb starting pitching, and I was now pitching every six days, and because of the National League-style of play that made it common for starting pitchers to be removed in the seventh inning for a pinch-hitter and a relief pitcher, I did not get the chance to finish games as I had in the American League.

Baseball was not fun to me anymore, so at the age of thirty and coming off a World Series winning team, I stubbornly quit the game.

I went home for a few weeks and thought long and hard about what I had done and why I had reacted this way.

I realized how much I truly loved to throw a baseball. I thought about signing my first professional contract with scout Jesse Flores with a $15,000 bonus and the thrill that came with putting on the uniform for the first time and seeing the joy in my parents' eyes when I used the money to buy them a car, refrigerator, and stove.

I also faced the hard truth that even though I loved the game, I thought about how my attitude became very negative and about how hard I had been on myself. I thought about how I reacted to my performance that year versus the team's success, and then I recalled games when we lost 1-0, and I would spend time thinking about what more could I have done to have won the game.

It took this time period and these circumstances to realize there is only so much you can control, and if I was going to be successful as a big league pitcher, my attitude was in need of a major adjustment.

At this moment in my life, I made a commitment to myself, from that day forward, to have an unwavering positive attitude in everything I do.

Immediately, I was more aware of the life lessons that were there for the taking every day at the ballpark and stayed with me during my twenty three year pitching career. And I have that positive attitude to thank for my becoming more fearless and determined on the mound.

My determination to embrace a positive attitude started at the ballpark, but it did not end there. I began studying at the Garden Grove Community Church with Dr. Lyle Schaller and embraced his teachings on how a positive attitude can free yourself from being afraid to fail.

Prior to this experience, my attitude allowed me to run from my problems and blame others, but the attitude adjustment and the lessons I learned during this time proved to be real to me as long as I believed in myself first. I was, for the first time, able to trust in what I was doing and truly believe I could succeed. Without believing in myself, I had no choice but to fail, and that's essentially what happened to me in Pittsburgh.

Life is just too short to fail.

To be successful in anything in life, you can't be afraid to fail. I look at the game of baseball as a great learning tool for life because you have the opportunity to succeed and fail on a daily basis, and facing this with a positive attitude prolonged my career.

My career lasted twenty three years, and I went on to fully enjoy sharing a World Series championship with my teammates on the Minnesota Twins. I also personally enjoyed 287 career victories and 60 complete game shutouts and learned to maintain a positive attitude through my losses as well.

Scout: Jesse Flores

- AVG .328 • Hits 3,010 • Runs 1,513
- Boston Red Sox 1982–1992, New York Yankees 1993–1997, Tampa Bay Devil Rays 1998–1999
- All-Star: 1985–1996
- Silver Slugger Award: 1983, 1986–1989, 1991, 1993–1994
- Gold Glove Award: 1994–1995
- Elected to the National Baseball Hall of Fame: 2005

WADE BOGGS————————•

I had my own style of play that I needed to perfect to become successful.

When I was drafted out of high school by Boston Red Sox scout George Digby in 1976, I was one step closer to my dream of making the major leagues.

Little did I know it would take me six minor league seasons before I reached the big leagues. During that time in the minors, I was repeatedly told that I would never play third base in the big leagues because I was too slow and I could not hit for the power that many third basemen of the time possessed.

I never really listened to the criticism because I believed in myself. I had my own style of play that I needed to perfect to become successful. I did realize that there were players more talented than me who did not make it, so I dedicated myself to being prepared mentally and physically for any opportunity I had to make it to the majors—no matter how long it took.

Throughout my time in the minors, I filtered the values and work ethic I learned growing up in a very strict military household to my discipline of growing my abilities as a hitter.

This discipline and dedication served me well when I finally got my first call-up to the big leagues in 1982. Even though I was excited to be a part of the Red Sox, I was in a role backing up starting third baseman Carney Lansford and was limited to a pinch hitting opportunity every tenth game or so.

While it would have been easy to get caught up in the mix of emotions, I took that same discipline to my preparation—even if I was not going to be playing every day. Because of my lack of playing time and Carney being the everyday third baseman, I was driven by the fear of being sent back to the minors, so I made the commitment to myself to be mentally and physically prepared for each game as though I were the starter.

This proved to be a very smart move because Carney broke his ankle on a road trip in Detroit. I instantly went from bench warmer to starting third baseman. Thanks to my dedicated work ethic, I was prepared to take advantage of this opportunity and be ready to play at my highest level.

Understanding this lesson in those first few weeks of being a starter, I took this attitude every day of my career that once I made it to the big leagues, your work is just beginning, and you have to work even harder every day to stay there.

I was surprised when I got to the big leagues and even later as a hitting coach that there are chronic complainers who don't want to put the extra work in to stay on top.

For me, it was simple. Once you become successful and know how to maintain consistencies and successes, it becomes easy because there's a drive, and most of your great ballplayers never get complacent.

You have to want to be the best and drive to work at it every day.

Scout: George Digby

- AVG .239 • Home Runs 3 • RBIs 106
- Pittsburgh Pirates 1963, Houston Astros 1965–1968, Montreal Expos 1969–1971

R O N   B R A N D

Have you passed along what you learned to anyone else?

In 1960, I was twenty one years old. I had just finished another season in the Pittsburgh Pirates' minor league system, and I was contemplating ending my baseball career.

That winter I really gave some serious thought to what I wanted to do. I had a regular job in the offseason, but I wanted to stay in shape, so every afternoon after work I would head to North Hollywood Park with a bag of baseballs.

One day in the park, a man in his early thirties was carrying a bag with a bat and some balls. He asked me to work out with him. I jumped at the chance because I had no one to practice with me. He started throwing batting practice to me, and I was hitting the ball very well.

And then he stopped. He walked toward me and said, "You could be a pretty good hitter, but you are a small guy and you should try not to hit all those fly balls. Try to hit line drives."

I was taken aback. I thought to myself, "I am a professional baseball player—who is this guy?"

But I wanted someone to play with, so I did not argue. Instead, I asked, "What do you mean? I can hit line drives."

"Of course you can," he said. "But only when you concentrate. When you're in a game, you won't be concentrating enough, and you'll hit fly balls and be out."

We agreed to meet at the park the next day at 3:30. Instead of hitting, we ran around the park. Next, we worked off the tee. I hit the balls straight against a backstop. My natural reaction was to look up and see where the ball hit the backstop. He told me to stop looking up. "Instead of thinking about where the ball goes, think about where you hit the ball. Put all of your focus on that," he said.

I really started popping the ball, and I thought we'd had a good workout. But he told me we weren't done yet, and we began a series of sprints. We ran so hard that my knees began to shake, and I felt like I was going to get sick.

Every day for the next six weeks, we met at the same time and repeated those exercises He never gave me his phone number—just his name: Don Bussan.

Before I left for spring training, I finally asked him how he learned so much about baseball. He told me that he had failed as a ballplayer in the U.S. and went to Japan to play. It was there where he really studied the fundamentals of baseball.

When I left for spring training in 1961, I felt like King Kong. I did not share my workout routine with anyone when I arrived at camp. I wanted to see if they noticed a difference in me. In a few days, one of the coaches came to me and said I was ripping the ball and asked what had happened to me. I simply told him that I had done a lot of mental work, practiced the fundamentals, and focused on the simple parts of the game.

While I knew that my hitting had improved, I would have never guessed what else had improved. I had always run the 60-yard dash in 7.2 seconds. Now, I was routinely timed at less than 6.8 seconds.

I didn't make the big leagues that year, but I was sent to Kinston, North Carolina. The coaches pulled me into their office and told me that they had never seen anyone make so dramatic an improvement. They then did something I had never heard of a team doing. They tore up my contract. To show they recognized my work, they increased my salary from four hundred dollars a month to eight hundred dollars a month.

I made it to the big leagues in 1963. In my first game against the Los Angeles Dodgers, I was shagging flies during batting practice, and I heard a familiar voice in the distance.

It was Don.

He was just shouting, "Way to go!" He did not ask for a free ticket. He never asked for credit. His reward was simply watching me succeed. He was totally selfless.

I ended up playing nine years in the majors. For a guy with limited abilities, it was beyond my wildest dreams. I spent my post-playing days as both a manager and a scout, and I never forgot what Don and those six weeks meant to me. I used those drills repeatedly with other players along the way with the same passion he taught me to help them reach their potential.

In the late 1990s, I tracked down Don and called to say thank you.

"You have already thanked me, Ron," he said. "Have you passed what you learned along to anyone else?"

When I told him I had, he responded, "That's a better thank-you than any words you could ever say to me."

Scout: Ross Gilhousen

- AVG .305 • Hits 3,154 • Home Runs 317
- Kansas City Royals 1973–1993
- All-Star: 1976-1988
- American League Batting Champion: 1976, 1980, 1990
- American League MVP: 1980
- American League Championship Series MVP: 1985
- Lou Gehrig Memorial Award: 1986
- Elected to the National Baseball Hall of Fame: 1999

G E O R G E   B R E T T———————•

Are you willing to put in the hours to become a good hitter?

I was the youngest of four boys, and all three of my brothers—Bobby, John, and Ken—played professional baseball.

My family held me accountable, and that drove me to succeed in baseball. At El Segundo High School, I was one of six seniors who were selected in the baseball draft.

I was selected by the Kansas City Royals in the second round. The Royals were an expansion team, and it was a great opportunity to get to the big leagues very quickly.

I was promoted to the majors in two years, and during my rookie year, I struggled for the first time on the baseball field. I had always excelled at baseball, but I was really in a slump, but since I was a high draft pick, the Royals kept me in the big leagues to get experience.

At the end of the first half of the season, I was hitting around .200 and just could not seem to do anything right.

Our hitting coach Charley Lau did not spend much time with me, and I did not think too much about it at the time until he came up to me after the last game before the All-Star break.

He put his arm around me and said, "George, you don't know this, but I have been watching you very closely for about two months, and I have recognized that you have not made any adjustments. You are obviously struggling; why are you not making adjustments? I know you could be a good hitter, but it will take some serious work to break your habits. Are you willing to put in the hours to become a good hitter?"

I had nothing to lose at this point and said, "Yes."

Charley told me to be at the stadium early the next day, and we looked at film and started to work on basic fundamentals. We agreed that my goal would be to finish the season with a .250 average.

For the rest of the year, Charley and I took extra batting practice. We met at 3:00 on the road and 4:00 at home and worked intensely on fundamentals and adjustments every day.

A month later, I was hitting .250. I felt like we made it and wanted to celebrate. Charley saw it differently. He said the new goal was now .260. And when I reached .260, the new goal was .270. I was attacking the ball and just hitting at a different level, and I owed it all to those daily sessions and Charley. I had improved almost overnight.

Then, close to the end of the season, I walked into the locker room, and everyone's head was down. Charley had been fired.

I was crushed. I went hitless in my last twelve at-bats.

The Royals went through a few other managerial and coaching changes, and eventually Whitey Herzog was hired as our manager, and he brought Charley back as our hitting coach a few years later, and we picked up right where we left off with our sessions.

I often wondered why he waited until the middle of the season to work with me. I felt I could have hit .300 my rookie year, and he would have never been fired had we started with the sessions earlier.

One day, I asked him, and his response is another lesson I learned from him.

"George, I wanted to see if you could do it on your own, and you couldn't. You needed to hit rock bottom. People, especially young people, are not open to advice and change until they fail. I needed to have you fail so you would be open to change. If I would have talked to you about making adjustments in spring training, you would not have listened to me. Am I right?"

I nodded yes.

This life lesson of being humbled, along with all of the fundamentals he helped me with, changed me forever. I really believe if it were not for him, I would not be who I am today.

Scouts: Ross Gilhousen, Art Lilly, and Tom Ferrick

- Successfully studied for his medical degree during his eight-year career as a player with the New York Yankees (1946–52, 1954)
- Appeared in World Series: 1947, 1949, 1950, 1951
- Nicknamed "The Golden Boy" during his playing career
- President of the American League from 1984–1994

D R .   B O B B Y   B R O W N⎯⎯•

You have to listen to your heart to see yourself clearly.

I was always an ambitious person.

I was so ambitious, in fact, that I had two dreams: become a doctor as well as a professional ballplayer. It never occurred to me that I couldn't do both. I knew I couldn't play baseball forever. I couldn't see a reason not to do both.

At the core of being an ambitious person is believing in yourself, and when others would say "you can't do it," it would just drive me more because I had confidence in myself.

I was premed at Stanford University in 1942 when I turned eighteen, and like everyone else my age, I enlisted in the Navy. Our country was in the midst of World War II. I was called up to active duty in 1943. The Navy assigned me to medical school at Tulane, and the war ended in 1945. At that point, I was two thirds through medical school and had a greater sense of conviction in pursuing my dreams both on the diamond and in medicine.

The most important time for me in realizing my two dreams was when the dean of the Tulane University Medical School let me play baseball and be enrolled in medical school at the same time. Even though he approved it, he still couldn't believe he had a ballplayer in medical school, and he couldn't understand why I wanted to play ball.

At the time, in 1946, the dean was being paid one thousand dollars per month, and I told him the New York Yankees offered me a salary package that was significantly more than he was earning, and that convinced him to be more flexible.

If I were just in medical school or training to be a professional athlete, I would have to manage my time wisely. However, when I was doing both at the same time, I had to become an expert in time management as well as developing my athletic and academic skills.

I just knew I couldn't waste any time in the day in school or in practice to make everything fit in. I learned the skill of squeezing every ounce of life out of every moment and was experiencing full and complete days.

With my ambitious dreams, I was very fortunate because my parents were supportive and didn't doubt me. I think deep down, the people in baseball never thought I could do both, and medical school administrators did not believe it either.

Tulane and the Yankees gave me the chance to do both, but I also knew it drove them nuts.

There were days that I felt too that it was nuts. On the hardest of days of balancing both commitments, I can still hear my dad say, "Stay with it. Stay with it. You're going to make it."

I was doing well enough in school and in baseball to make me feel like I could do it. I knew if I really worked hard, I would make it, and those very simple words from my dad's heart lifted me up on the hardest of days.

I knew if I didn't go to medical school, I would be a better player and vice versa, but I needed to be true to myself, and I wanted both dreams to come true. You have to listen to your heart to see yourself clearly.

I never doubted I could do it. A lot people doubted me because I was doing something that had never been done before, and the world is filled with naysayers. The path to doing something that has never been done before for me was to listen to my heart and the loved ones who believed in me unconditionally. For me, I was able to block everything else out and manage my time properly. It's easy for everyone to be negative and to say I can't do it, but I felt I could hit anyone, and I felt I could pass at school.

And I did.

Scout: Joe Devine

- Wins 224 • Strikeouts 2,855 • ERA 3.27
- Detroit Tigers 1956–1963, Philadelphia Phillies 1964–1967, 1970–1971, Pittsburgh Pirates 1968–1969, Los Angeles Dodgers 1969
- Pitched a perfect game June 21, 1964
- All-Star: 1957, 1959, 1961–1964, 1966
- Elected to the National Baseball Hall of Fame: 1996

JIM BUNNING————————.

It was one of my happiest days on the mound ... because of the obstacle it symbolized in my own life.

I missed spring training the first three years I was under contract to play for the Detroit Tigers. Education was very important to my father, and I had negotiated a clause in my contract that allowed me to stay at Xavier University. After the spring semester ended each May, I would travel to wherever they assigned me to play in the minor leagues.

I earned a bachelor's degree in economics, and my first full year of professional ball was not until 1954.

The next two years I played in the minors, and I rightfully earned a reputation as a temperamental pitcher. The coaches told me I had a million-dollar arm and a nickel head. This made me furious at times, because I was probably the only one on the team with a college degree. But I realized my temper was holding me back from believing in myself as much as the coaches believed in me.

I was doing very well against right-handed hitters, but for whatever reason, left-handed hitters were hitting balls all over the place against me. I couldn't figure out what I was doing wrong. I was a sidearm pitcher, and the coaches kept trying to get me to throw over the shoulder. I tried it, but it just did not work.

I knew that part of understanding good advice is determining if it is right for you; throwing over the shoulder just was not right for me.

During the offseason of 1956, the Tigers sent me to Havana, Cuba, to play for a winter league team, the Marion Owls. I think the setting in Cuba—the weather and a different culture—mellowed me from the moment I arrived.

I met our pitching coach the first day. His name was Connie Marrero, and he took some time with me and taught me how to properly throw a slider with a sidearm motion. I finally understood what good advice really was because his advice was right for me.

Almost instantly, my whole repertoire changed. Thankfully for my coaches, my attitude did as well. I finally had a pitch that could get lefties out. From that moment on, I was more confident against both righties and lefties, and equally important, I didn't let my emotions get the best of me.

I returned to the Tigers in 1957. I didn't immediately start, but I knew my opportunity would come. In early May, I got the call to start against the Boston Red Sox. I faced Ted Williams, and I struck him out three times—every time with my slider.

It was one of my happiest days on the mound. Not just because I struck out arguably the greatest left-handed hitter ever, but because of the obstacle I had overcome to do it.

Scout: Bruce Knatcher

- AVG .328 • Hits 3,053 • RBIs 1,015
- Minnesota Twins 1967–1978, California Angels 1979–1985
- All-Star: 1967–1984
- Rookie of the Year: 1967
- American League Batting Champion: 1969, 1972–1975, 1977–1978
- American League MVP: 1977
- Elected to the National Baseball Hall of Fame: 1991

R O D   C A R E W————————————●

Dreams are really about pursuing a feeling.

I grew up in Panama, and one of my earliest influences was my Uncle Clyde.

He taught me a lot about dreams and how they become realities. He knew how much I wanted to play in the big leagues. He said, "Rod, if baseball's what you want to do, then go for it. Don't let anyone or anything get in the way of reaching your dream. I believe in you."

He continued by rattling off a list of distractions as if he were reading a roll call: "No girls! No drugs! No alcohol!" He closed by saying, "Just focus, Rod."

I was eleven years old then, and I had such a focus and concentration to play in the big leagues that I started playing with twenty-year-old men just to learn. At night, I would lie in bed and listen to baseball games on Armed Forces Radio.

Baseball was a wonderful escape for me as a boy because it gave me a passion to love. My home life was more devoid of love than most homes—my dad abused my mom and me, and baseball was my way out.

When I was at home, I felt scared. When I was on the field, I felt a peace about myself, and I pursued that feeling as much as anything. It was a very comforting feeling.

Dreams are an interesting concept. Talk of dreams commonly includes discussions about the pursuit of an activity or an accomplishment, but at the core, I believe they are really about pursuing a feeling. For me, hitting a baseball gave me the best feelings of my young life.

As great as I felt hitting a baseball, I did not have many friends off the field. With my home life being what it was, I was a very quiet boy, and I was always afraid to have schoolmates or teammates over at the house. I was afraid they would see my parents fighting. The positive side of being quiet and isolated was that it allowed me to have a deeper concentration on my dream of being a ballplayer.

The Minnesota Twins drafted me, and they sent me to the farm team in Wilson, North Carolina. The town was very small, and there was a lot of racial tension at the time. And the fans had a hard time rooting for black player from Panama.

I channeled my Uncle Clyde's advice and added another distraction that I would not allow to impact me: unruly fans.

Each day in Wilson, I would hold my head up and focus on my dream. In Panama, I felt safe on the field—it was my escape. In Wilson, I had nowhere to escape. The ball field itself was not a safe place. There were four brothers in the stands that were in my face all year long. They yelled some of the most horrible, demeaning, and racially charged statements you can imagine. And they were there for every game.

As much I tried to follow Uncle Clyde's advice to stay focused, it was hard because they were so determined. They were so loud, and it just never stopped.

But I never responded to them. I chose instead to hear my Uncle Clyde telling me, "Don't let anything stand in the way of what you really want in life."

During the last game of the season, the brothers said to me they were going to wait for me after the game by the locker room door.

I was so scared. I came out of the locker room with my chin up like I was preparing for a fight. Just like they said they would be, they were there.

Before I could say anything, one of the brothers said, "As much as we rode you all season long, we wanted to apologize. You're the best player we've ever seen."

I calmly exhaled, and this response came out: "You don't have to apologize to me. I was here to play ball for the Twins, and I didn't hear a word you said."

Not only did I get promoted the next year, but those four brothers became my friends. The brothers later lived in Baltimore, and they would come see me play when I played against the Orioles.

All of these outcomes were gifts from staying true to my dreams and not letting anything or anyone get in my way.

Scout: Herb Stein

- Home Runs 324 • RBIs 1,225
- Montreal Expos 1974–1984, 1992, New York Mets 1985–1989, San Francisco Giants 1990, Los Angeles Dodgers 1991
- All-Star: 1975, 1979–1988
- All-Star MVP: 1981, 1984
- Gold Glove Award: 1980–1982
- Elected to the National Baseball Hall of Fame: 2003

G A R Y   C A R T E R

I thrived on versatility and the power of embracing a positive attitude all the time.

The day I was drafted in the third round by the Montreal Expos changed my life in two major ways. First, I had moved one step closer to my dream of playing in the big leagues. Secondly, the scout who signed me, Bob Zuck, told me my best path to the big leagues would be as a catcher.

Now, up until this point, I had spent my childhood and high school career as a first baseman, pitcher, and shortstop, but my passion for the game that I learned from my father, Jim, and my older brother, Gordon, was greater than my passion for a particular position.

My mindset was that I was a baseball player first. Not a catcher. Not a first baseman. Not a shortstop. A baseball player. Anything I could do to improve my chances to play and to learn would only benefit me in the long run, so I listened intensely to Bob's recommendation. I knew Bob had my best interests in mind. He saw something in me, and I trusted him.

After being drafted, the Expos assigned me to the Gulf Coast League so I could begin to learn a new position. Most of the credit of my development as a catcher in the early days goes to the Expos catching coordinator Bill McKenzie. Bill took me in and started to develop techniques, and I started to follow big league catchers a lot more intensely. He worked with me relentlessly at blocking balls and learning the mental nuances of my new position.

During this time, I struggled with the new position, but I would not let anything deter me from reaching my potential. All I could ask for in life was an opportunity, and I knew I had to prove my worth constantly. Learning to be a catcher was just another obstacle. I began to thrive on versatility and the power of embracing a positive attitude all the time.

I credit versatility and a positive attitude as much as anything for my reaching the big leagues. These two skills helped me when I showed up to report for my first major league game on my birthday, April 8, 1975, and manager Gene Mauch tossed me an outfielder's glove and told me I was playing right field.

Without Gene's confidence in my talent and his understanding of versatility, I know I would have either been on the bench or back in the minors. Just like in the Gulf Coast League, I focused on being a ballplayer more than any position, and of my 144 games, 90 or so of them in my rookie year were in the outfield. I made the All-Star team that year, and our All-Star manager, Walter Alston, put me in another new position: left field.

Over the next two years, a series of manager changes with the Expos had me playing catcher and positions in the infield and outfield. It was not until 1977 that I became a full-time catcher in the Big Leagues just as Bob Zuck had predicted when I was still in high school.

I would have never imagined at the beginning of my career that I would go on to catch 2,056 games at the major league level. All I knew then was I needed experience any way I could get it. The attitude to do whatever I could do to keep learning is what I will forever credit my longevity and success to.

Scout: Bob Zuk

- AVG .297 • Home Runs 379 • RBIs 1,365
- San Francisco Giants 1958–1966, St. Louis Cardinals 1966–1968, Atlanta Braves 1969–1972, Oakland Athletics 1972, Boston Red Sox 1973, Kansas City Royals 1974
- Rookie of the Year: 1958
- All-Star: 1959–1964, 1967
- American League MVP: 1967
- World Series Champion: 1967, 1972
- Elected to the National Baseball Hall of Fame: 1999

ORLANDO CEPEDA———.

I began to learn compassion for other people and for myself.

Even though I'd had a lot of success during my baseball career and made a lot of money, I had never truly found happiness during my playing days, and it showed in the poor decisions I made off the field.

In the early 1980s, I hit rock bottom.

My playing career had ended, and I had just lost a job as hitting coach of the Chicago White Sox. I spent some time in prison. I lost all of the money I had earned as a ballplayer. Baseball writers were saying that even though I had performed at a Hall of Fame level on the field, my off-the-field actions would keep me from Cooperstown. I had become distant from my wife and my four children, and my relationship with them was severely threatened.

Then I did something that would change my life forever. I finally saw myself not as the public saw me but as my total self: the good and the bad. This was the tool I needed to find to finally grow in the right direction and stop making poor life decisions.

Looking back on my baseball career, I realized how much I struggled to make the right decisions. I often cracked under pressure when I was faced with choosing between right and wrong. I made a string of poor decisions, and now I fully realized the damage I had caused myself, and—equally important—how to change my path.

I began to learn compassion for other people and for myself. It was a humbling experience to recognize that money and success had changed me, and I had to learn to change for the better.

I took out a small piece of paper and wrote down what I wanted from my life from that day forward. I wrote about my desire to do what was right no matter the circumstance, to be true to my family every day, to use my name in baseball to make a difference in the lives of others, and—if I made the Hall of Fame—to use that honor to make an even greater difference.

I tucked that sheet of paper away and began using it, and my newfound devotion to Buddhism, as a map of my future. I kept the list a secret, even from my family. I wanted to just do the right thing and let the positive vibes flow from my actions.

Armed with the commitment to myself, I made the decision to begin following through on my promises. I moved my family to California and started looking for a job in baseball.

At the time, I had to support four kids and a wife, and I had no money. I went to people I could trust: the San Francisco Giants. I went to work for them, and I started rebuilding my life and following the list.

More than fifteen years later, I had forgotten about the list. Then, one morning in January 1999, I got the call from Cooperstown saying that the Veterans Committee had elected me to the Baseball Hall of Fame.

After sharing the news with my family, I found the list and opened it. I realized that the impossible is possible if you go in the right direction.

All of my dreams came true, including finding true happiness for myself.

Scout: Pedro Zorilla

- AVG .269 • Home Runs 282
- Cincinnati Reds 1984–1991, 1996, Los Angeles Dodgers 1992–1993, Detroit Tigers 1993–1994, Baltimore Orioles 1997–1998, St. Louis Cardinals 1999–2000, San Francisco Giants 2001
- All-Star: 1987, 1989
- Silver Slugger Award: 1987, 1989
- Gold Glove Award: 1987–1989

ERIC DAVIS——————•

Play the game the way you know how to play, no matter
what the circumstance.

I was twenty-two years old when I started my first season in the majors. Pete Rose was my manager. It was quite a unique situation because he was both a teammate and our manager, but he was the first one that really instilled confidence in me.

He told me, "Never let anyone tell you what you can or can't do."

It was about this time that he moved me from cleanup hitter to the leadoff spot. At the time, everyone wanted me to be a leadoff hitter because I had speed. One game, I noticed the third baseman was playing deep, and I dropped a bunt to try to take advantage of my speed, but I popped it up for an out.

When I got back to the dugout, Pete came over to me and said, "Rookie, next time you attempt a bunt, I'm fining you one hundred dollars." I was shocked because lead-off hitters are supposed to get on base.

He then responded and said, "Son, do you have the ability to get a run with a bunt? You have the God-given ability to hit the ball out of the park, so why would you waste that pitch when you could hit it out of the park?"

I didn't realize it then, but his whole mentality was to teach me something that seems so simple but is hard to understand. This lesson is simply to play the game the way you know how to play it, no matter what the circumstance. If you approach the game with no restrictions, he said, that is the path to staying true to yourself and reaching greatness.

This lesson of staying true to myself was one that was reiterated to me again at about the same time from Dave Parker. Dave was starting his first season with the Reds that year but was a proven veteran and one of the great players of the game at the time.

He stopped me in spring training and said to me in the way that only veteran players can speak to rookies, "You're going to be my caddy all through spring training. Stick with me, kid, and I'll teach you things."

As great as a ballplayer as Dave was, he also had made some poor decisions with drug use, and he told me, "Don't look at what I've done, but look at what I'm doing."

This was Dave's approach to life and the game, and he constantly stressed to me, "Always be true to yourself. If you are true to yourself, then you are true to the game."

It was like Dave and Pete were conspiring together to teach me a lesson, and it was working because I was performing well in the leadoff spot and was contributing with power instead of pure speed.

About that same time, I met Willie Stargell for the first time. Willie had retired from his playing days with the Pittsburgh Pirates and was with the Atlanta Braves as a coach. He pulled me aside during batting practice and gave me tips on hitting. He stressed to me to have slow feet and quick hands. Willie went as far as to tell me, "In hitting, just like in life, if you can slow things down, everything will become clearer to you. When you slow the game down, you actually possess the power to speed it up."

Those three encounters during my rookie year laid the foundation for me. I learned that year how to be receptive to listening and then take that knowledge and adapt it to life to be the best me I could be—both on and off the field.

Scout: Larry Barton, Jr.

- AVG .288 • Hits 2,042 • Home Runs 223
- Boston Red Sox 1937–1951
- Drove in 100 runs or more six times
- All-Star: 1941–1944, 1946–1948, 1950–1951
- Elected to the National Baseball Hall of Fame: 1986

BOBBY DOERR

Focus on building steps and what is right in front of you.
Everything else will work itself out.

Growing up during the Depression in Los Angeles, my first memory was bouncing a ball off the front porch for hours on end.

As an eight-year-old at the time, it was the only form of entertainment I had. However, looking back, it was great practice for my destiny as a ballplayer.

I grew up dreaming of big league ballplayers. My bedroom walls were plastered with pictures of Mickey Cochrane, Jimmie Foxx, and Billy Herman.

About the time I became a teenager, I told my dad that I wanted to be a professional baseball player when I grew up.

Now, a lot of children tell this to their dads, but I think my dad's reaction, more than anything, is what propelled my dream into a reality.

He sat down and looked at me square in the eye and said with a serious tone, "Son, I believe in you and anything you set your mind to. If you really want to play ball, don't make it just a dream. Make a commitment right here and now. You commit to working hard and don't ever miss practice. I'll take extra work and mow lawns so you won't have to work for extra money for the family, and you won't be distracted with anything. You can just focus on your dream."

Now, you have to remember, this was in the middle of the Depression, and every child my age was doing their part with odd jobs to contribute to the family's income. My dad worked for the telegraph company. During very hard times, he volunteered to work only three days a week, even though his status allowed him to work five days a week and earn more money, so that other dads could get some work too.

He had a hard life. However, he never let it get in the way of loving me, encouraging me, and doing the right thing no matter what the situation.

His support and commitment to me was such a big help because it allowed me just to focus on one thing: baseball. I started playing American Legion baseball when I was fourteen, and by the time I was sixteen, I was offered a contract to play for the Pacific Coast League team in Hollywood.

Even though I was focusing on my dream, there were times when financial troubles were so intense that I would say prayers at night, hoping that our fortunes would turn around. My dad heard me say these prayers and told me not to be distracted. He reassured me everything would be fine if I just worked at what I could control.

He encouraged me, "Focus on building steps and what is right in front of you. Everything else will work itself out. I believe in you."

My first break came when I got the chance to play for the team in Hollywood. I played with them from June 1934 until the winter of 1935, when I had a chance to move to San Diego and play there. That's where I met Ted Williams for the first time.

He was 6'3" and 150 pounds soaking wet. Ted was standing by the batting cage the first time I saw him. I watched him enter the cage, and he ripped about five solid line drives. I remember two things about that day. One was the sound his bat made when it made contact with the ball. It was so pure and natural and sounded different from what I had ever heard before. The other was overhearing an older player saying that we should sign this tall, skinny kid immediately. Before I knew it, I was standing at the railroad stop, and Ted came skipping towards me, and he told me the Boston Red Sox had signed him. He was my teammate from that day forward.

With Ted as my teammate and my father's wisdom engrained in me, I had turned those dreams into reality just like my dad said I would.

Scouts: Eddie Collins and George Stovall

- Scout for Chicago White Sox
- General Manager: Montreal Expos 1988–1991, Florida Marlins 1993–2001
- President/CEO/General Manager: Detroit Tigers 2001–present
- World Series Champion: 1997, 2003

DAVE DOMBROWSKI———•

I soon saw a vision for myself to pursue a career as a
Major League Baseball general manager.

As an accounting major at Western Michigan University in the mid-1970s, I wrote a class paper chronicling the responsibilities and challenges of being a general manager of a major league team.

Throughout my research, I attempted to talk by telephone to as many general managers as I could to get a first-person account of the job. At the end of each interview, I asked the same question, "Can I meet with you in person?" During the process of researching the paper and talking with these executives, I soon saw a vision for myself to pursue a career as a major league general manager.

One of those general managers was Roland Hemond of the Chicago White Sox. Upon meeting Roland, I asked him about the skills needed to become a general manager and his thoughts on the best approach for me to get my first job. He told me that all the clubs send their general managers to the Baseball Winter Meetings, and I should go there and meet with as many clubs as I could.

I mailed letters to every team with hopes of getting the chance to spend some time with them at the meetings. The meetings were in Hawaii that year, so for a few months I saved every penny I could and convinced a friend of mine to come with me for support and a vacation.

During that time, I basically received a rejection letter for every letter I sent. While the response was not what I had hoped for, I left for Hawaii with spirits high and hopes of meeting as many baseball people as I could to realize my dream and launch my career.

The first few days were filled with pleasant exchanges with the clubs in the lobby and promises to meet one-on-one during a specific time only to have all of them fail to show up when they said they would.

I was pursuing my dream and was just getting rejected repeatedly.

Toward the end of the weeklong meetings, I was sitting in the lobby of the hotel with my head hung low, and Roland saw me. I told him my experience, and he instructed me to meet him the following morning at 8:00 a.m. because the White Sox might have a job opening.

By this point, I was totally dejected and was not surprised when Roland later said he could not meet in the morning but said to come up to his room at 1:45 that afternoon.

I went to the beach with my friend and sat there in my swim trunks, contemplating not only whether the dream of being a general manager, let alone working in baseball, would ever happen. Time had passed, and I went up to my room in my swim trunks and called Roland's room, expecting fully to have him reschedule again like so many other. To my shock, he wanted me to come right up. I explained to him that I had just come back from the beach and needed to change, and he said not to bother.

So, in flip-flops and wet swim trunks, I took the elevator to Roland's room for my first job interview in baseball.

The interview started in Roland's room, but I was quickly whisked away with White Sox farm system director Paul Richards, who gave me a walking interview on the trade show floor.

I left Hawaii feeling good about the experience and ironically was greeted with a standard rejection letter from the White Sox upon returning home.

After returning home, I went to Comiskey Park and met with Mike Veeck, and he offered me a job for seven thousand dollars a year, and after some haggling over my salary and deciding to complete my degree via correspondence work, I took the job on the spot and began living my dream as an employee of the White Sox.

Looking back now after having been a general manager for several teams, I remember repeatedly, especially that day on the beach, questioning my dream. The drive for my dream is what kept me going, and even with the countless rejections, I am thankful that I stuck it out.

It is a lesson of perseverance that I draw on constantly because it taught me never to give up and that something, whether it is a job or the search for a new player, always opens up if I want it badly enough and am willing to be patient.

- Wins 197 • Saves 390 • ERA 3.50
- Cleveland Indians 1975–1977, Boston Red Sox 1978–1984, 1998, Chicago Cubs 1984–1986, Oakland Athletics 1987–1995, St. Louis Cardinals 1996–1997
- Pitched no-hitter May 30, 1977
- All-Star: 1977, 1982, 1988, 1990–1992
- World Series Champion: 1989
- Cy Young Award: 1992
- American League MVP: 1992
- Elected to the National Baseball Hall of Fame: 2004

DENNIS ECKERSLEY⸺.

I realized that talent had gotten me into the big leagues but perseverance would keep me there.

From as far back as I can remember, I was a competitor.

When I was a young boy, I kept competing against the older kids until I felt like I was the best of the group. I would tag along with my old brother Glen and his friends, and I learned a ton from him. I did all I could to keep up with them, and it drove me to obsessive levels. Once I became this way, I would move on to the next level and repeat the process again.

This was a lesson I learned from my dad, who told me simply, "Believe in yourself! No one is better than you until they prove it."

As a young boy, I needed that. Every child needs to hear that.

This approach propelled my growth until I was about sixteen years old, and there was no next level until I graduated high school and could sign with a professional team.

Looking back, this approach was both good and bad for different reasons.

The good part was it accelerated my baseball abilities and fueled a level of competitiveness and desire that was the foundation for my career. By the time I made the big leagues, I had this cockiness and confidence about me that sustained me. I was probably a bit scared deep down inside, but when you are afraid, you get angry, and it drove me and served me well.

However, I realize now I rushed things, and baseball stunted my growth a bit as a human being. I created an extreme personality that stretched my talent.

Twelve years into my career, I came to accept that I had an alcohol problem.

For the first time, I looked at myself in the mirror and saw myself for who I really was, and it hurt.

I started in the big leagues when I was twenty years old and never grew up. At some point in every man's life, his problems catch up with him. This was what was happening to me, and my talent was being wasted. I realized how unhappy I was as a person. I was living on a fuse and had all of this talent but did not know how to control it.

Alcohol was my escape.

I had a problem with alcohol, and that was part of my story.

I realized that talent had propelled me to the big leagues. Alcohol could have ended my career, but instead, perseverance kept my career alive.

It was during this time I joined the Oakland A's, and I became a relief pitcher. My confidence had served me so well throughout my career, but now, my confidence was coming down to acceptance. It was a demotion for me to go to the bullpen, and I had to swallow my pride. I had to accept who I was and where I was in life, just like I needed to accept my problems with alcohol.

I learned to recognize the good and bad equally in life, and acceptance was the key to my success. The fire that was in my belly since I was a little boy was burning as hot as ever, and being sober and focused brought a new level of competitiveness that only comes with maturity and life experiences.

Becoming a relief pitcher brought that out in me, and it was like I was reborn. Now I could attack batters, and I couldn't do that as a starter. I felt like I was a kid again on the mound, attacking my brother's older friends through my pitches.

Through the good and bad times, I had passion.

I was consumed with passion. I'd go to bed and think about baseball. I'd dream about baseball. I know I was successful in this game because I was passionate.

I can't see doing it any other way.

Scout: Lloyd Christopher

- Wins 266 • Strikeouts 2,581 • ERA 3.25
- Cleveland Indians 1936–1956
- All-Star: 1938–41, 1946–48, 1950
- Led the American League in strikeouts: 1938–41, 1946–48
- Led the American League in wins: 1939–41, 1946–47, 1951
- American League Pitching Triple Crown: 1940
- Elected to the National Baseball Hall of Fame: 1962

BOB FELLER————————•

Every day is a new opportunity.

I grew up on a farm in Marquerite, Iowa, during the Depression.

Even during those hard times, we were never destitute because my father was a very successful farmer regardless of what was happening in the world around us. He worked hard to make sure he was a success. My mother was just as dedicated. She was a schoolteacher, a nurse, a newspaper correspondent, and a school board member.

They were hard working people, and their drive and leadership by example influenced me tremendously at an early age.

This drive, from as far back as I can remember, was to do one thing: be a baseball player.

My dad had been a semiprofessional pitcher when he was younger, and he encouraged me not only with his words but more importantly with his actions.

He built a pitcher's mound and set up a home plate between the house and the barn. I remember spending hours every day throwing pitches to my dad and building my arm strength. When it was too cold in the Iowa winters, we'd keep throwing inside the barn.

By the time I was twelve years old, we built a whole baseball field on the farm complete with a grandstand, and we started a team. With me as a pitcher, dad would charge spectators 35 cents to come and watch as another sign that his innovative and hard work paid off.

At this time, I was growing stronger and could feel my fastball increasing its speed. There were some games that more than a thousand people would come to see me play—including major league scouts.

One of them worked for the Cleveland Indians, and I signed as a teenager and immediately was assigned to the big league club.

In my first start, I struck out fifteen batters against the St. Louis Browns, and we won 4-1.

My life changed overnight, but my dad taught me that every day is a new opportunity, whether you are a farmer or a ballplayer, and I never looked to the past. I always looked to tomorrow and tried to do with my life what my dad did with his. This approach was simply to work hard and build on successes and learn from failures.

That's the way life is, with a new day every day. It is exactly the way baseball is with a new game every day, too. My dad and mom always looked ahead, and that's the approach I took with my career and my life.

Scout: Cy Slapnicka

- Wins 114 • Saves 341 • ERA 2.90
- Led the American League in saves: 1977–1978, 1981
- Cy Young Award: 1981
- American League MVP: 1981
- Elected to the National Baseball Hall of Fame: 1992

ROLLIE FINGERS

Even though I was not getting results, I wanted it so bad and refused to quit.

I was eighteen years old when I signed with the Philadelphia Athletics in 1964. I gave my dad three thousand dollars, bought my mom a sewing machine, and bought a 1956 Chevy.

I thought I was on my way.

It all happened so quickly that by 1971 I was already worried that I was on my way out of baseball. By then, I had pitched three years in the big leagues with the Oakland Athletics and was failing miserably.

I earned a spot in the rotation again in spring training, but for some reason I could not get anyone out. I don't think the first three months of the season I lasted beyond the third inning if I even made it that far. My earned run average was up beyond 5.00, and I was a sitting duck.

As it was the case in those days, our manager Dick Williams threw me into the bullpen as a mop-up guy. For pitchers, being the mop-up guy was just a nice way of saying that they were keeping you around until they could find a way to send you down to the minors.

I tried to keep my chin up with the demotion and promised myself to keep working and prepare for the next opportunity to restore Dick's confidence in me and return to the rotation again.

One day we were playing the New York Yankees in the type of game that seems to last forever. We were down eight runs and used up most of our pitchers while trying to get through the game. Our offense somehow climbed back into the game, and we took a 13-11 lead late in the game. Dick called down to the bullpen. The only people that were left there was the pitching coach and me. As much as I had been struggling, he had no other choice but to put me in.

I was called from the bullpen with the game on the line, and it felt completely different. I earned my first save, and the next night he put me in the same situation, and I earned another save.

After the game, Dick called me into his office. A few days earlier, being called into his office would have surely meant he was releasing me or sending me down to the minors had it not been for this simple twist of fate. Dick told me I was doing a good job and was throwing hard with good control and was going to be his closer or, although in those days, we called them "stoppers."

On a very simple level, this opportunity was really a consequence of being in the right place at the right time, but I also never stopped working at it. Even though I was not getting results, I wanted it so badly and refused to quit.

That was right around the All-Star Break. I had seventeen saves by the end of the season, and my life and my dreams had been redirected.

As time went by and I became a full-time closer, I started to mature and understand why this role fit my demeanor and personality more. I liked the idea of not knowing when I was going to pitch. Now, instead of having four days to wait for the next opportunity or four days to think about the last game, I just would come every day prepared to compete and wait for the phone to ring.

I liked entering pressure situations and thrived under the competition. I never wanted to hear the national anthem from the pitcher's mound ever again.

It was a great life experience to know that I was not nervous coming into games and gained confidence in these situations where I had lost it as a starter. The more confidence I gained through success, the more of an advantage I felt like I gained against opposing hitters. Sometimes I was so confident that I felt like I had one strike against the hitters before they entered the box.

From that moment on, my confidence just grew stronger, and I took control and never let anything get in my way in my new role.

Scout: Art Lilly

CAREER HIGHLIGHTS

- Wins 236 • ERA 2.75 • Strikeouts 1,956
- New York Yankees 1950–1967
- All-Star: 1954–56, 1958–61, 1964
- Led American League in wins: 1955, 1961, 1963
- Led American League in ERA: 1956, 1958
- Cy Young Award: 1961
- World Series MVP: 1961
- Elected to the National Baseball Hall of Fame: 1984

W H I T E Y   F O R D_____•

I still marvel at how fast life can change.

When I was in high school, I went to an open tryout with the New York Yankees in April of 1946.

I was a first baseman and dreamt about being the next Lou Gehrig for the Yankees.

What kid didn't have this dream?

My dream didn't seem to be a reality because at 5'9", 180 pounds, I had virtually no shot of playing professional baseball. At the tryout, I played first base during infield practice, and then each of us got five swings in the batting cage.

I must have not done very well because Paul Krichell, a Yankee scout, came over to me and said, "I don't think you'll make it as a first baseman, but I liked your arm motion and the way you threw the ball around the infield. Have you ever thought about pitching?"

I told him I never had thought about it because I wanted to be like Gehrig, but I would be willing to give it a chance.

Paul spent about fifteen minutes with me and showed me how to throw a curveball. He wrote some tips down on a piece of paper. His list included how to hide your hand in the glove, how to grip the ball, and how to follow through. It was very simple stuff, but I had never known it, so it was new to me. I soaked it all in and figured I would give pitching a chance.

A month later, I finished high school, and our sandlot team went 36-2 and won the championship game at the old Polo Grounds. We won 1-0 in 11 innings, and, armed with my curveball, I pitched the entire game.

A bunch of scouts were there and started offering me contracts. The New York Giants offered me a three thousand dollar bonus. The Brooklyn Dodgers offered five thousand dollars, and the Yankees upped their original offer of five thousand dollars to seven thousand dollars.

Four months earlier I had never pitched before, and I signed a contract to become a pitcher for the Yankees, and my entire life changed in four months.

My first visit to Yankee Stadium, I went over to warm up, and I got such a kick out of warming up that I threw the first pitch towards the screen. By September of 1946, I was putting Paul's advice to use and was throwing my curveball during a playoff game for the Yankees.

I still marvel at how fast life can change. I'm so grateful I was aware of the moment when the gateway to my dreams opened up that day.

Scouts: Paul Krichell and John Schulte

- Genovese signed thirty-five players, who became major league players. Some of the most notable are as follows: Bobby Bonds, Jim Barr, Jack Clark, Royce Clayton, Chili Davis, Rob Deer, George Foster, Ken Henderson, David Kingman, Garry Maddox, Gary Mathews, Sr., Randy Moffitt, Gary Ryerson, and Matt Williams.
- The Professional Baseball Scouts Foundation presents the George Genovese Award at its annual dinner to a scout who has had an outstanding career.

GEORGE GENOVESE.

I'll never forget that feeling of wearing that clean, white jersey for the first time. It was one of the happiest moments of my life.

Like any kid, I was interested in sports, and baseball was by far my favorite.

By the time I was a teenager, I was a batboy for my older brother's team. Seeing them up close made me feel I had the potential to be a professional prospect.

This was in the late-1930s, and scouts could sign you in high school at the time. I wanted desperately to play professional baseball, but I also knew that I needed to finish high school and earn my diploma.

I waited to finish school as a lot of my friends signed contracts to play professionally. I went to a couple of tryout camps and was not getting the recognition I felt I should. Every camp was the same. I was told that I was too small, and I was usually cut the first day. I didn't let it discourage me, and I kept seeking as many opportunities to play as I could.

The following year in 1940, I was playing in a Catholic summer league, and the director of the league told me that the St. Louis Cardinals were having a tryout camp and I should attend.

This all sounded great, and like the earlier camps, I was not going to let anything get in my way. The only hurdle I faced this time was financial, as I only had twenty-five cents and needed some extra money. I borrowed the money from my brother and begged him not to tell Mom and Dad what I was doing.

I drove the four hours to Waterbury, Connecticut, with a friend who was also trying out, and we spent the night in the car because we could not afford a place to stay.

This camp felt different from the start, and it showed in the result. Even though there were about five hundred guys there, I made it past the first day.

That was the good news. The bad news was that I had $1.25 to my name, and we were told that we couldn't sleep in the car.

For food, we found a White Castle and ate five-cent burgers. A worker there told us there was a farm up the road and we could sleep there. We met the farm owner, and with our stomachs full of sliders and our dreams higher than ever, we slept in his barn.

We did that for four days, and on the fourth day, my friend was cut. This was sad for two reasons. First, because he was my friend, and secondly, he was also my ride home.

I told Roy Dissinger, the scout that was running the camp, that my friend was my ride home and said if he planned to cut me like the other teams had, then please go ahead and do it because I have no place to stay and no ride home.

He kind of smirked at me and said, "Son, go to the team hotel and get a room. Charge your meals and your room to me. We want you to stay."

For the first time, someone else was acknowledging my dream.

The camp ended a few days later. Roy told me he would be in touch, and he even offered me money to get home. I was so excited to get home that I did not even take my uniform off and hitched a ride with a truck driver who was heading to New York for the World's Fair.

My parents surprisingly were not upset with me, and within a few days, the Cardinals sent a telegram with a contract for eighty dollars a month to start playing with their farm team in Hamilton, Ontario.

That was the start of my career, and I thought I was on my way to the majors.

After playing a few years in the minors, I received my draft notice in 1942 and was inducted into the Army Signal Corps and served my country in Okinawa until 1946.

Upon returning, I started right back in the minors and felt like I was back at tryout camps and proving myself once again to get a shot to play in the big leagues.

Just like in the summer after high school, I persevered and put everything into it I could. On April 29, 1950, after the journeys to the tryout camps, being stationed in Okinawa, and many years in the minors, I got to wear a Washington Senators jersey.

I'll never forget that feeling of wearing that clean, white jersey for the first time. It was one of the happiest moments of my life.

Scout: Roy Dissinger

- Wins 124 • Saves 310 • ERA 3.01
- Chicago White Sox 1972–1976, Pittsburgh Pirates 1977, New York Yankees
  1978–1983, 1989, San Diego Padres 1984–1987, Chicago Cubs 1988,
  San Francisco Giants 1989, Fukuoka Daiei Hawks 1990, Texas Rangers 1991,
  Oakland Athletics 1992–1993, Seattle Mariners 1994
- All-Star: 1975–1978, 1980-1982, 1984–1985
- Yankees career leader in ERA (2.14) and hits allowed/9 IP (6.59)
- Elected to the National Baseball Hall of Fame: 2008

RICH

"GOOSE" GOSSAGE———.

I remember pumping my fist in the air and pointing to the
sky, and I just screamed, "This is for you Dad!"

As far back as I can remember, my dad always told me that I would grow up to be a big leaguer.

Now, I know a lot of kids hear this sort of talk from their parents, but I grew up in Colorado in the 1950s, and the big leagues might as well have been on another planet as far as I was concerned. My dad was a die-hard Yankees fan, and players like Mickey Mantle and Whitey Ford were like cartoon characters to me because they were larger than life. It seemed so far away to me, but that didn't stop my dad from dreaming for me.

Dad died when I was a junior in high school, but Mom was there to carry the torch as my biggest fan. After he died, I missed him terribly, but the dream of being a baseball player took on a new life and made me feel closer to him.

By my senior year in high school, I had scouts starting to show up at my games, and I started to feel confident in what my dad had dreamt for me.

One of the scouts was Bill Kimball of the Chicago White Sox.

One day, I pitched a complete game and the very next day was asked to pitch an inning and a third, and I was just so tired that I gave up six runs. It was one of the worst outings of my life, and of course, that was the game that all the scouts were watching me.

I really thought I blew my chance and thought I was done.

We grew up without a lot of money, so I knew after I finished high school that I would have to get a job. The day of my graduation, I applied for and got a job coaching kids in high school through the local park district, and I came running home to tell Mom the good news, that I would be able to help support the family.

I was so surprised when she said there was another job for me to consider too, and there was a man in the living room that would explain more about it to me.

I walked into the living room, and there was Bill.

He said he knew the reasons that I pitched so poorly that day. He told me how much he believed in me and that he was in our living room because the White Sox would like to offer me a contract.

I signed on the spot.

I was so excited and scared to death at the same time. I missed my dad terribly because I was achieving his dream and wanted to share it with him and get the kind of advice that only a father can give a son. After Bill left, I borrowed my brother's Jeep and drove to a favorite spot in the mountains where dad used to take me.

When I got there, I was so overcome with emotions that I just cried.

I didn't know anyone could cry like this. It was the emotion of achieving my dad's dream. It was the thought of missing him and not sharing it with him. I was also scared because I thought about pitching against all the guys I grew up idolizing. I knew I was good in Colorado, but I had no idea how I would do on the next level. I could not imagine getting a guy like Mickey Mantle out.

I sat there by myself and continued to cry all day long and wondered if I'd done the right thing.

Before I knew it, in the blink of an eye, I was playing in the rookie league and decided that I would not be afraid. I promised myself that I would pursue my dream and my dad's dream with all my heart. I made a commitment to myself not to look back, and I would put aside any and all apprehension I had and move forward with the complete confidence in myself that my dad always had in me.

In the minors, I learned from Ray Berres, Sam Hairston, Johnny Sain, and Chuck Tanner, and before I knew it, White Sox general manager Roland Hemond let me know that I would be joining the big league club.

As fate would have it, my first game was against the Yankees at Yankee Stadium. When the bus arrived, the veteran players went to the locker room, and I just drifted for a bit. I met a security guard who directed me towards the dugout. I followed the light through the dark tunnel and all of a sudden boom!

The feeling of seeing an empty Yankee Stadium was a lot like the feeling I had the day sitting on the mountain crying and thinking of dad.

My life, I thought, had come full circle, and it was the greatest feeling I've ever had.

That night, as fate would have it again, I got into the game. I threw my warm-up pitches on the mound, and I just stood there in awe of the moment. The umpire actually came and said something to me, but my legs were shaking so badly that I don't even remember what he said. I'm sure I was delaying the game or something, but it did not matter because I had reached my dream.

As he walked away, I remember pumping my fist in the air and pointing to the sky, and I just screamed, "This is for you, Dad!"

Then, I turned around and fired my first major league pitch and never looked back just like I promised myself and how my dad always knew I would.

Scout: Bill Kimball

- Wins 170 • Strikeouts 1,778 • ERA 3.29
- New York Yankees 1975–1988
- Holds Yankees single season record for strikeouts: 1978 (248)
- Led the American League in wins: 1978, 1985
- All-Star: 1978–1979, 1982–1983
- Cy Young Award: 1978
- Gold Glove Award: 1982–1986

R O N   G U I D R Y————————•

I don't think you're ready to quit.

I got called up to the New York Yankees in 1975 and finished the season with the big league club. I thought I had pitched well in the situations that they put me in, but it was not in the role I had wanted.

In Class AAA ball, I was a closer.

Now, with the big league club, I was in a bit of a Catch-22 because Sparky Lyle was our closer, and he was the best in the game at the time.

I obviously wanted to pitch, but I felt like I would never have an opportunity to do what I felt I was born to do. Those thoughts dominated my mind throughout the offseason.

I made the big league club in 1976. One day, I was boarding the bus, and our manager, Billy Martin, asked me to come to the front of the bus. He said they are sending me down because they just got Bucky Dent and a pitcher in a trade. Because of this, they had to send me down again because they would be over the twenty-five man limit. Billy consoled me and reassured me that I was in their plans and that I could one day lead the league in saves.

This pattern seemed to repeat itself.

I would be sent down for some reason that always seemed to be beyond my control and then return to the big league club only to be behind Sparky and then shipped down again. It is very tough to keep your confidence level high when you are down there, and I really started to feel that the Yankees did not believe in me as much as I believed in myself.

The other challenge was the competition at Class AAA was becoming easy for me. I was worried I was losing my competitive edge even if I could actually jump over Sparky to become the closer.

Surprisingly, one day Sparky and Dick Tidrow, another Yankees pitcher, came up to me and told me that the only thing I needed to set myself apart and stay with the big league club is a breaking ball. It would, they said, complement my fastball nicely and set up my other out pitches perfectly.

I was willing to take Sparky's advice, but I thought it was very interesting and wondered why he would help me because he knew I wanted his job.

He must have read my mind because he looked at me and said, "If you're better, kid, then the club is better. Got it?"

I didn't say a word to him. I just kind of nodded, and to this day, I still wonder how he knew what I was thinking in that moment.

Under Sparky's guidance, within two months, I learned how to throw the slider. I knew I was ready with my new pitch in tow, but opportunity was still not knocking on my door to use it in a game.

After forty-five days of not getting into a game, I was in the bullpen that night.

After the game, Claude Boyle said the team was sending me down, and the reason was because I was not pitching.

I had worked so hard to learn the new pitch and was so upset because the reason I was not pitching was because they were not pitching me.

For the first time, I really wanted to quit. I was so hurt with the thought I'd be quitting the thing that I loved the most.

He said he understood what I was saying and said he knew I could do the job, but I just needed to be patient. I was through being patient. I thought to myself that I'll just go back to Class AAA and pitch, and a few weeks from now, I'll be back sitting in the bullpen in Yankee Stadium.

To make things more difficult, my wife was pregnant.

I went home after that conversation and told her to pack her bags because we were going to back home to Louisiana.

She didn't say much.

It was very quiet on the way home to Louisiana. We had driven that highway many times. She knew where the turnoffs were, so about five miles before we reach I-80 near Harrisburg, Pennsylvania, she pulled the car over and knocked some sense into me and said, "I don't think you're ready to quit. I've known you for a long time, and this is the first time I've known you to quit anything. If you really think you can't pitch in the big league, then let's drive home. If you know you can do it, let's turn this car around and drive back to Syracuse so you can continue on with your dream. If it just takes one more chance to do it, then it's worth it."

I sat there for a second, and without saying a word, we turned the car around.

Two days later, I pitched for Syracuse, and within a few weeks I was back in New York.

As Billy and Claude had said, opportunity was finally aligned for me. Because of a trade, our club was in need of a starting pitcher. I was still frustrated and just wanted a chance to pitch and did not care at this point if it was as a reliever or a starter anymore, so I volunteered to fill the spot on the team and be a starting pitcher.

In no time at all, I was a permanent fixture of the rotation with my breaking ball pitch a big part of my success, and I even won the Cy Young Award two years later.

I've learned that so much in life is to listen to what others—especially those that care about you like Sparky, Dick, and my wife—are telling you. If I had been a hard-headed person, my life would be totally different, but with time, caring people, patience, and dedication, you can pursue anything in life.

Scout: Atley Donald

●─────────────────────────────C A R E E R   H I G H L I G H T S

- AVG .273 • Home Runs 325 • RBIs 1,163
- Detroit Tigers 1963–1977, Texas Rangers 1977, Cleveland Indians 1978, Oakland Athletics 1978, Toronto Blue Jays 1978, Seattle Mariners 1979–1980
- All-Star: 1965, 1968, 1970, 1973
- World Series Champion: 1968

WILLIE HORTON———.

Even though the world around me was filled with people saying what I couldn't do, I started to believe what I could do.

I was born the youngest child in a family of twenty-one children.

As you can imagine, this made for an interesting time, but to make it even more challenging, we also grew up in the projects. My parents did the best they could, but there were many hard obstacles we faced.

Growing up poor, all you have sometimes is your imagination and your dreams. When I was about thirteen years old, for the first time, I started to think my dream of being a baseball player and getting out of the projects could actually be a reality.

This thought inspired me, and I dreamed more seriously and began to visualize my dreams more clearly. Even though the world around was filled with people saying what I couldn't do, I started to believe what I could do.

My parents recognized this in me too and made an extremely difficult decision.

They let me go.

Well, sort of. I went and lived with the Keefes. They were friends with my dad, and they lived in a much nicer and safer neighborhood with better schools than where I was living. The new environment seemed to be filled with people who told you that you could do anything.

From that day forward, I had two sets of parents, and it gave a great focus to my determination and dreams. This determination and inspiring environment carried me through a great high school baseball career and into the Detroit Tigers farm system.

Before I could blink, I was playing in Class AA Knoxville, and that is when, for the first time in a long time, I struggled. I was not doing well at the plate, and I missed home.

I needed to hear supportive and encouraging words, so I called home to my dad and told him what I was feeling.

He just lit into me pretty hard. I remember him using some rough language on me and telling me I was a coward, and he just hung up on me. I was already scared about what I was doing before the call.

Now I was just frightened.

I sat there and was so mad at my dad. I wanted some comforting words, and all he did was yell at me. As I sat there, I wondered why he reacted that way. I started to understand that I had a greater responsibility as a ballplayer than just to myself. I thought about my parents. I thought about all my brothers and sisters. I thought about the Keefes. I thought about the Tigers and the opportunities they were giving me.

I went to the ballpark the next day, and everything clicked. Before I knew it, the Tigers had called me up to the big leagues, and that was the next time I would see my dad.

He came to the game late in the season of 1963. I was twenty years old, and in my second at-bat, I hit a home run against Robin Roberts, and all the pressure and responsibility just glided off of me as I circled the bases and smiled.

I remember thinking to myself that it is very wise to listen to people who care about you because they see more in you than you see in yourself. That, for me, was the key to growing up.

Even though I thought I had grown up by then, this realization again proved very valuable to me about ten years later.

I was still playing for the Tigers, and Billy Martin was our manager. I was having an okay year. Billy told me I was fading a bit physically and that with age, you can't rely on your talents and have to work at it.

Like my dad always had done, Billy was giving me tough love, and I loved him for it.

At that time in my career, my production really had started to drop. I could have taken the easy way out and retired, but I was fortunate that I was armed with a deep understanding of people and the art of tough love.

This lesson drove me my entire career. A career that started on a high note thanks to my dad ended on a high note thanks to Billy.

Scout: Lou D'Annunzio

- General Manger: St. Louis Cardinals 1964–1966, Cincinnati Reds 1967–1977
- President: Cincinnati Reds 1973–1978
- World Series Champion: 1964, 1975, 1976

BOB HOWSAM————————•

It takes a lifetime of experience and a wonderful wife to truly understand the difference between enjoyment and appreciation.

When I came out of the Navy after World War II in 1947, I returned to Denver and took a job as the executive secretary of the Western Professional Baseball League. A short time afterwards, the Class A Denver Bears baseball team was for sale, and I convinced my dad and brother to pool everything we had and buy the team.

I did not realize it at the time, but I was living my dream.

How lucky was I that I owned a baseball team in my hometown with my family? The future looked bright for Denver and baseball, and I was excited to be a part of it. After we failed to turn the Bears into a major league team, we led the league in attendance over many years and eventually helped create the Continental League in 1959.

We knew we needed to build a larger stadium than the thirteen thousand seats the original Bears Stadium (later called Mile High Stadium) could hold, so we added seats. To help add to the bottom line, we also decided to start a football team as a charter franchise of the American Football League.

This team was the Denver Broncos.

Unlike the perception of today's owners or even the owners of the time, our family did not have a lot of money. We just had a love of the game. Due to financial reasons, we were eventually forced to sell both the Bears and the Broncos. All of the owners beside me were very rich people whose living, unlike mine, did not depend on profits from their teams. This realization was one of the true low points of my life, as I was faced with the reality of my financial limitations and lost the two teams that had become such a part of me.

I was too young to realize it at the time, but I learned so much from this low point because I found greater determination, more strength, and the ability to move forward regardless of the challenges I was facing. I learned that when everything is easy, you do not appreciate success as much. It taught me a lot about who I was as a person. It gave me the wherewithal to know how to overcome anything by staying focused on success and understanding what was really important to me.

Looking back, however, that low point of having to sell both of the teams I loved so dearly turned out to be one of the best moments of my life. And I have an unwavering positive attitude and the love of my wife, Janet, to thank for it.

Not long after this challenging time in 1964, I received a call from Branch Rickey, who was serving as an advisor to St. Louis Cardinals owner August "Gussie" Busch. Branch encouraged Mr. Busch to talk to me about becoming the team's general manager and replacing Bing Devine.

I remember being so excited about the thought of working in baseball again and telling Mr. Busch that I was very interested, but I needed to talk with my wife.

Without any hesitation, Janet said to me, "You've always loved baseball, and I'm glad to see you have this opportunity. Let's do it."

With those words and a strong wife at my side, I accepted the position. I realized more than ever that day how much Janet meant to me. Because of her being a tower of strength, I could survive any of the low points. Even after such a tough time, I was able to turn it around again, and I owe so much of that and my future success to her.

I joined the Cardinals halfway through the season, and the team turned it around quickly. We won the World Series in my first year. Because of everything I had been through in Denver, I was able to truly appreciate my success in St. Louis. I was also more grounded than ever before because I was humbled so greatly in Denver. This life lesson, combined with the love of Janet, helped me tremendously because my time in St. Louis was short lived, as the Cardinals returned to a .500 ballclub in my first full two years with the team, and many Cardinal fans resented me because I had replaced a popular general manager.

The opportunity arose for me to start fresh with the Cincinnati Reds as their general manager in 1966, and again with Janet's support, we departed to Ohio.

During my eleven seasons in Cincinnati, I was able to build a team that became "The Big Red Machine" and experienced back-to-back World Championships in 1975 and 1976.

I am thankful to my wife and for the life lessons in Denver, as I was able to not only enjoy the success we experienced in Cincinnati but to truly appreciate it.

And it takes a lifetime of experiences and a wonderful wife to truly understand the difference between enjoyment and appreciation.

- MLB AVG .293 • MLB Home Runs 99 • MLB RBIs 443
- Negro Leagues: Newark Eagles 1938–1942, 1946–1948
- Major Leagues: New York Giants 1949–1955, Chicago Cubs 1956
- National League RBI champion: 1951
- All-Star: 1952
- World Series Champion: 1954
- Elected to the National Baseball Hall of Fame: 1973

M O N T E I R V I N———————————•

It has been a very rewarding way to live, and I am grateful that I listened to that wonderful man on that day.

As a young African American boy, I did not aspire to be a major league player because African American baseball players were not allowed to play in the big leagues.

As an eight-year-old, I had a lot of energy and was always running and jumping. One of my teachers told me that rather than throwing stones, I should turn my energy to organized sports. I started out as a soccer player and then got involved in football, basketball, track, and baseball. By the time I got to high school, I played every sport I could.

That's when I met Jesse Miles. Jesse was the head of a local youth sports club, and in his high school days, he had been something that I aspired to be: a four-sport star.

We would have long talks, and I would ask him questions about life, sports, and his experiences. I listened to every word he spoke. I remember him telling me, "In order to be successful, you have to play hard, play clean, and play fair. And not just on the field, but in your daily life."

Those words would remain with me every day of my baseball career and my life.

The first time those words helped me was when I was in high school. I ran into a lot of prejudice even then, but I wouldn't let it deter me because I knew I could play fair—even when others did not.

I hit .686 for my high school team. One of my teachers knew a major league scout and told him about me: "If they ever want to integrate baseball, this is the guy. He's big, strong, and smart."

I didn't know it at the time, but my teacher convinced the scout to watch me play. But this was in 1936, and it would still be eleven years before Jackie Robinson broke the color barrier.

Jesse's words served me well because I understood the rules of the day, and I played fair and clean. I went to play in the Negro Leagues before I eventually joined the major leagues and the New York Giants in 1949. Joining the Giants was quite a moment because as a child, the possibility of playing in the major leagues was not even a dream.

All of the advice that Jesse had given me served me well in everything I have done. It has been a very rewarding way to live, and I am grateful that I listened to that wonderful man on that day. His instructions made a difference in my life.

Scout: Alex Pompez

- Wins 284 • ERA 3.34 • Strikeouts 3,192
- Philadelphia Phillies 1965–1966, Chicago Cubs 1966–1973, 1982–1983, Texas Rangers 1974–1975, 1978–1981, Boston Red Sox 1976–1977
- All-Star: 1967, 1971, 1972
- Led the National League in strikeouts: 1969
- Cy Young Award: 1971
- MLB Comeback Player of the Year Award: 1974
- Elected to the National Baseball Hall of Fame: 1991

FERGUSON JENKINS

You can never get enough advice and knowledge.

My mom was always my number one fan, and she continually stressed to me, "You can never get enough advice and knowledge."

I didn't want to fail at anything I did, so I listened intently and took her words to heart for the rest of my life.

This proved to be a very wise decision, as my destiny started to manifest when I was about fifteen years old. I started developing physically, and scouts began to turn up more and more when I was pitching.

I grew up in Canada, where hockey is the national sport, and like most kids in Canada, I spent a lot of my time playing hockey. Up until then I was an athlete, but I was about to become a pitcher.

It took me some maturity to understand the difference, and I realized the distinction thanks to a mentor. Gene Dijera was a scout and, for me, a tutor who taught me how to throw. Like a lot of young athletes, I think I was blessed with natural ability, but that is not enough. I even had it a little harder since I did not grow up in America, playing baseball daily. I was a tall and lanky kid who had the natural ability but needed to learn the nuances of pitching.

I think my desire grew stronger with my body as I eventually shot up to 6'5". As both my height and heart for pitching grew, so did the scouts' interest in me.

I spent the last two summers of high school working at every aspect of the game. When I wasn't practicing, I would beg my dad to drive us south of the border to Detroit to Tiger Stadium. For me, watching big league players was a life lesson in itself. We talked about the time required, and I realized at this time that dreams take hard work. He told me there were thousands of other high schoolers like me who were in the stands and wanted the same dream. Therefore, I had to work harder.

While I wanted to talk to the players on the field, I couldn't get access to them, so I did the next best thing. I thought back to my mom's advice of always getting more advice and knowledge. I watched them and tried to just learn from observing, and it really paid off in my development.

The Philadelphia Phillies signed me, and all that hard work was worth it.

Now, instead of watching the ballplayers from the stands, I was one of them. And I kept doing what I did in the stands, but now I had a front row seat. I would watch my teammates like Jim Bunning, but now I could combine my observations with questions to them directly. The knowledge I gained from teammates like Jim had a tremendous influence on my mechanics and my mental approach.

I felt there was a pattern in my life that went back to Gene and all those trips to Tiger Stadium with my dad that was repeating now that I was in the big leagues. It was the notion that the path to success was through emulating others who are successful at what you want to do.

And the skill of learning how to learn was the greatest knowledge I ever acquired. It had a lasting effect on my career.

Scout: Tony Lucadello

- Chicago White Sox 1962–63, 1966
- Hillerich-Bradsby Silver Bat Award: 1956
- Career at-bats: 49
- Hitting coach: Houston Astros 1976–1982, San Diego Padres 1984–1988
- Member of the Ithaca College, Appleton, Wisconsin, and Westchester County Sports Halls of Fame

GROVER
"DEACON" JONES———•

Those words and that moment have stayed with me my
entire life.

Baseball has always had a way of making me feel special, and I also felt destined that my life would have a special impact on the game of baseball.

In 1951, as a young man, I was on a team that was playing for the American Legion World Championship, and I was voted the best American Legion player in the United States.

As part of the honor, I was recognized in the National Baseball Hall of Fame in Cooperstown. The distinction was prior to naming Brooklyn Dodgers legend Jackie Robinson as a member in 1962 and was the first time a colored ballplayer was featured at the Hall of Fame.

With the honor came a lot more attention, and in those days, there were no player drafts, so the teams held extended player workouts for prospects to play alongside the club's big league players and decide which amateur players they wanted to sign.

The Brooklyn Dodgers invited me, as an eighteen-year-old, to come to the tryout camp. The invitation brought me closer to my dream of playing big league ball and also the opportunity for me to play with and meet my hero: Jackie Robinson.

I was sitting on the dugout bench one day during camp when Mr. Robinson came over to me, and we started talking.

"Grover," he said.

"Yes sir, Mr. Robinson," I replied.

"It's your last day, and you are a good ballplayer, but you are only eighteen years old, and you are going to college, right son?" he said.

Little did he know, but I was fighting with my parents at the time about their desire for me to go to college and delay my dream of playing professional baseball.

I could fight with my parents, but I couldn't with Mr. Robinson.

"Yes sir, Mr. Robinson," I said.

"Good," he said. "I'll see you in four years."

He proceeded to tell me how difficult professional baseball would be for a man of color. I had grown up in a loving family in a safe cocoon and did not realize how disappointing racism could be. He continued by telling me that an education is a strength that no one could ever take away from me. He said I should never let any person prevent me from pursuing my childhood dream and that a solid education is a foundation to fully reaching my dream.

Those words and that moment have stayed with me my entire life.

I left the camp and put my dream of playing professional baseball on hold and took a scholarship to play baseball at Ithaca College, thinking that I would see my hero again in four years.

It proved to be a little sooner.

Three years later, my college baseball team was traveling through Atlanta, and we were in the airport. Someone alerted us that the Dodgers were in the airport, and I was determined to go see Mr. Robinson.

I pushed my way through the crowd and touched him on the shoulder and said, "Mr. Robinson, You don't remember me, but ..."

He interrupted me and said, "Of course I remember you, Grover. Did you get your college degree?"

I gave him an update on what I had been doing, and shortly thereafter, armed with my college degree, I signed my first professional contract to play with the Chicago White Sox.

During my second year of pro ball, we were playing the Dodgers in a spring training game, and I hit a ball off of Sandy Koufax and slid headfirst into third base and heard a loud pop in my arm.

The injury hurt so bad, and I couldn't throw the ball from first base to home plate. I was a right-handed thrower, and I became so desperate that I even tried to throw left-handed. I cried my eyes out to my wife and told her I would not quit even though physically I could not play anymore.

Thankfully for myself, I had listened to Mr. Robinson and earned my college degree and was prepared to still pursue my dream of being in baseball. This experience provided me with the strength and awareness to be prepared for the inevitable cycle of life of dreams, disappointments, and renewals.

My renewal came in the form of a series of opportunities that opened up for me thanks to my baseball knowledge and academic achievements.

The first opportunity was as a coach with the Appleton Foxes. From there, I was able to hold positions ranging from coach to scout for many other major league teams.

Despite all of the physical shortcomings I encountered, I was able to become what I wanted to be, and that was simply to have a special impact on the game of baseball.

Scout: Joe Holden

- Wins 283 • ERA 3.45 • Strikeouts 2,461
- Washington Senators/Minnesota Twins 1959–1973, Chicago White Sox 1973–1975, Philadelphia Phillies 1976–1979, New York Yankees 1979–1980, St. Louis Cardinals 1980–1983
- Gold Glove Award: 1962–1977
- All-Star: 1962, 1966, 1975

J I M K A A T——————————————•

Everything I have ever accomplished all started with my dad.

Everything I have ever accomplished in my career started with my dad.

I had the perfect dad for an aspiring athlete. He never pushed me or put pressure on me when I was a boy. He never said, "You need to do more than you are capable of." He encouraged me and helped pique my interest in sports.

I played basketball in high school, and I remember one game when I had a great game and scored a lot of points. I was expecting my dad to praise my game. Instead, he singled out one of my teammates: "Carl threw you some great passes tonight!"

He often humbled me in this way, and it was critical to my development as a pitcher. I was always learning to be the best I could be.

On the other hand, if I had a bad night, he would encourage me by saying, "You did a good job on defense."

Both types of comments helped me become not just a big league pitcher, but a man. And they were critical to me when I was being courted by scouts.

The Milwaukee Braves were very interested in me, and the Chicago White Sox said they would give me a twenty five thousand dollar bonus to sign. This was more money than I ever dreamed of, and it equaled about six years of my dad's annual salary. However, the major leagues required any player who received a bonus of more than four thousand dollars to spend their first two seasons on the big league club.

After he learned this, my dad did what he always seemed to do: the right thing.

He knew I was not ready, as an eighteen-year-old kid, to be playing in the big leagues. He felt I could benefit from training in the minor leagues and growing as both a pitcher and a person. With my dad guiding me, I signed a contract for four thousand dollars with the Washington Senators and went to the minor leagues to learn how to be a big league pitcher.

It was the best decision for me.

In those days, I had no idea what other players made. I collected baseball cards, and I wanted to be a big league ballplayer. That was all

I knew and all I cared about.

When I was assigned to the farm team, Cookie Lavagetto, the Senators' manager, told me, "Kid, you'll be on our staff in three years." I could not wait to tell my dad about it. But when I did, he gave me some humbling advice: "He might say that to every kid to encourage them. You need to show him that he's really right."

In 1958, I was in Missoula, Montana, and I led the league in just about everything. I wasn't trying to be a big league pitcher. I just competed at the level I was at, and I stayed in the moment. It all was because of my dad, who taught me to stay on an even keel.

Years later, I asked my mom if Dad ever said anything when I was younger about my potential as a pitcher. She said my dad had told her that he knew I had talent. "Let it happen," she remembered him saying all the time.

It was the proper way, in my mind, to handle a child athlete.

Through my dad, I learned to respect coaches, but I also learned to be my own coach when Johnny Sain said to me, "Learn what is best for you."

I followed Johnny's advice for the rest of my career as a ballplayer. Thankfully, my dad had taught me what was best for me as a person.

Scout: Dick Wiencek

- AVG .297 • Home Runs 399 • Hits 3,007 • Fielding Percentage .987
- Detroit Tigers 1953–1974
- Youngest player ever to win a major-league batting title, at twenty years old
- Played 242 consecutive games without an error
- All-Star: 1955–1967, 1971, 1974
- Gold Glove Award: 1957–1959, 1961–1967
- Elected to the National Baseball Hall of Fame: 1980

A L   K A L I N E————————•

I can't help but think my dad had a lot to do with my success by teaching me his wisdom and aligning the stars for me in the way that only a father can.

Growing up, I was quite shy. I was not a very ambitious boy who would go after goals, but my dad was always there to encourage me and support me.

I grew up outside of Baltimore in an area near where Camden Yards is today. As a teenager, with my dad's backing, during the summer I signed up to play in semipro baseball league that required me to play games five days a week and doubleheaders on Sundays.

Because it was summertime, there was one week where it was so very hot. It was so hot that I wanted to miss the Sunday doubleheader so I could go to the beach with my friends and hang out in the water and cool off a bit.

My dad reminded me that I made a commitment to play on this team, and if I missed the game, I would be letting down my teammates and breaking my promise to them.

It was at this moment that I first learned the meaning of commitment and felt a sense of responsibility.

These games were great for me because I was one of the younger players on the team and was competing against guys in their twenties and thirties that were much stronger than my teenage body frame and were much more experienced in the life lessons that dad was trying to teach me.

During this time, it was obvious to my dad that I was beginning to develop potential and skills as a ballplayer, and scouts started to take notice, and they were calling my dad all the time.

I honestly didn't know how far I'd go, but I felt that if I kept going at the pace I was at, I would have a chance to sign a contract.

My dad realized this before I did.

I never really thought about playing professionally until this time, and that lesson of commitment that I learned earlier came back to me again, and I put all my focus and energy my senior year into baseball.

I can't emphasize the experience of playing in a semipro league. I was a boy playing with and learning from men.

It was part of my dad's plan to bring me up that way. Dad taught me to learn to respect elders and live my life with pride and commitments and work for all I achieved.

This lesson served me well again when the scouts came calling with offers when I graduated high school. A number of teams offered bonuses that were great offers and that meant that I would enter the big leagues right away.

My dad, as always, had a different plan for me and as usual it turned out to be the right plan. In the midst of all those phone calls, he had developed a relationship with Detroit Tigers scout Ed Katalinas, and he was someone that earned my dad's respect. The Tigers also offered a bonus that meant I would start in the big leagues immediately.

I signed pretty much at that moment with the Tigers even though a lot of teams offered more money. My dad always said that he wanted me to start my career off right and felt that Ed really cared about me. He wanted me to grow and build, and did I ever. By the time I was twenty years old, I had won a batting title in the big leagues. I can't help but think my dad had a lot to do with my success by teaching me his wisdom and aligning the stars for me in the way that only a father can.

Scouts: Ed Katalinas and John McHale, Sr.

- AVG .306 • Hits 2,054 • RBIs 870
- Philadelphia Athletics 1943–1946, Detroit Tigers 1946–1952, Boston Red Sox 1952–1954, Chicago White Sox 1954–1956, Baltimore Orioles 1956–1957
- Eight consecutive .300 seasons: 1946–53
- All-Star: 1947–54, 1956–57
- Led the American League in hits: 1950–51
- Elected to the National Baseball Hall of Fame: 1983

GEORGE KELL

As it often turns out in life, if you are open to your surroundings, you can realize you are in the right place at the right time.

I signed my first pro contract with the Brooklyn Dodgers when I was eighteen years old, but my dad would not let me play pro ball until I finished at least one year of college.

After that year of school, the Dodgers sent me to a short-season Class D minor league team in Arkansas, and I did not do too well.

The next year I had a full season and hit .312, and the Dodgers promoted me to Durham, North Carolina. It all happened so fast. I was so excited to be promoted, making another step towards the big leagues. The Dodgers sent me a train ticket to North Carolina, and I traveled all night from Arkansas and joined the team the next day.

As fast as that seemed to happen, my life was about to take an even bigger turn three weeks later.

Along with about fifteen of my teammates, the Dodgers released me, and I was cut very suddenly.

The feeling was as if all of my dreams had turned into nightmares overnight.

Not only did it look like I would never play ball again, but to make matters worse, I was broke. I had no money and was a thousand miles away from home. I called my father, and he had no money either. I was stuck—literally.

The other guys who were released all took jobs at a military plant in Durham to make a paycheck for a little while. I remembered wondering how they could give up on baseball. I was not ready to give up on my dreams of being a ballplayer just yet.

When they tried to get me to join them at the plant, I told them, "Thanks guys, but no thanks. I'm a ballplayer."

As it turns out often in life, if you are open to your surroundings, you can realize you are in the right place at the right time.

I would soon realize how very fortunate I was to be stuck in Durham.

For the next few days, I sort of snuck into hotel rooms with some of the other ballplayers who were still on the team and slept where I could until I could think of a plan.

Thankfully, that plan was arriving by Lancaster, Pennsylvania.

The Class B Lancaster team came into town, and as luck would have it, they needed a few extra players—specifically a third baseman, which was my position!

I signed that day and joined the team immediately, and now armed with a second chance, I capitalized on every opportunity that came my way. I hit .299 that year, and the next season I led the league with a .396 average and earned a silver bat for having the highest batting average in all of minor league baseball.

Then, once again, my life changed quickly. This time my dreams did not turn into a nightmare. They were about to become reality.

While in the minors, Connie Mack came down in September and walked into our locker room. It was like God walking into the clubhouse. It got so quiet, and he said, "Mr. Kell, I'm Connie Mack. Would you like to play for Philadelphia?"

I didn't hesitate at all and quickly replied, "You bet!"

He told me he had just purchased my contract and wanted me to report immediately after I was done with the playoffs.

It was in all these moments that I felt that I was always touched by an angel. But then, all throughout my life, I realized we all are touched by angels, but it's up to us to listen to them. For me, the road to listening and recognizing angels was through my heart. I never gave up on my dreams even when it seemed that my dreams were giving up on me.

I was the most unlikely prospect in the world, and somehow I made it to the majors and the Hall of Fame.

Scout: Tom Greenwade

- AVG .256 • Home Runs 573 • RBIs 1,584
- Washington Senators/Minnesota Twins 1954–1974, Kansas City Royals 1975
- Hit 40 home runs in a season eight times
- Ninth player to hit 500 career home runs
- All-Star: 1959, 1961, 1963–1971
- American League MVP: 1969
- Elected to the National Baseball Hall of Fame: 1984

H A R M O N K I L L E B R E W—.

A positive attitude and believing in myself were the keys
for me.

I grew up in a very small town in Idaho with four thousand five hundred people.

I was very close to my dad growing up. He was a great athlete himself, and he encouraged me to play all kinds of sports as a young boy. He did not raise me to try to turn me into a professional athlete; he just wanted to teach me to do my best.

This attitude followed me through high school, where I played both football and baseball and loved both sports. The University of Oregon offered me an athletic scholarship to play football and be their quarterback. I accepted the scholarship, and at that point in my life I chose football mainly because it gave me the chance to get an education.

The summer after my high school graduation, I still played baseball with a semiprofessional team mainly just to stay competitive and do something.

One day, unbeknownst to me, Idaho Senator Herman Walker talked to Clark Griffith, a friend and owner of the Washington Senators, and recommended that they sign me to a contract.

I told them initially, "Thank you very much, but I want to go to Oregon to play football."

The Senators had other ideas.

The team sent Ossie Bluege to watch me play, but the game was delayed because of rain. It kept raining, and I thought the game would be cancelled, but eventually the sun came out. When we started to play, I hit one out of the ballpark, about four hundred feet. It was the first time I ever hit one that far, and I knew my destiny had now changed.

In those days, anything more than six thousand dollars was considered a bonus. Clark authorized a six thousand dollars a year contract and a four thousand dollar bonus, which meant I was going directly to the big leagues.

My first experience in a big league game seemed to happen almost immediately after that rainy day in Idaho. It was at Comiskey Park against the Chicago White Sox.

I got on first base in my first at-bat and somehow made it to second base with Nellie Fox standing right by me. I took a second to look around, and there were all these guys I had read about my whole life.

I was in heaven, but the moment did not last long.

After two years of bonus play in the majors, I was sent down to Charlotte and even farther down to Chattanooga. While this was technically a demotion, it was exactly what I needed. I started really clubbing home runs there and gaining confidence.

I finished the season in the minors with a batting average above .300 and was with Washington the rest of the year.

My career took off from there.

Looking back now, I know that a positive attitude and believing in myself were the keys for me. I learned this from Ossie. He always had a positive attitude and made me feel good, and his influence was a part of every home run I ever hit.

Scout: Ossie Bluege

- AVG .213 • Home Runs 44 • RBIs 198
- Chicago Cubs 1956–1958, 1960–1961, Cleveland Indians 1962–1964, Minnesota Twins 1964–1965
- Member of the American Baseball Coaches Association Hall of Fame
- Longtime manager of the University of Arizona baseball team

JERRY KINDALL

I realized the sacrifice my dad was making for me on so many levels. I never forgot that stance of integrity my father showed that day.

When I was in high school in St. Paul, Minnesota, in the early 1950s, I started to get some attention from scouts. It was like a dream come true for me for a number of reasons.

I loved baseball and dreamed of being a professional baseball player. I also dreamed of making a good living to help my family, and I felt like baseball was my chance. I was the oldest son, and I came from a very blue-collar family. My dad worked two jobs doing physical labor, and my mom was confined to a wheelchair with multiple sclerosis.

My parents were more concerned with my earning a college degree and being the first member of our family to go to college. They also understood the opportunities that baseball presented me and saw my passion for it.

I earned a scholarship to play both baseball and basketball at the University of Minnesota, and I played there for two seasons. The opportunity to work on my degree pleased my parents, and the chance to play baseball under coach Dick Siebert was going to get me closer to my dream of playing in the big leagues.

In those days, there was not a draft like there is today, and there were no rules against leaving college early. Teams were free to sign players at their discretion. The only exception was that if a bonus to a player exceeded four thousand dollars, the player was required to spend his first two years with the big league club. This rule was designed to prevent the larger-market teams from outbidding all of the other teams and stocking their minor league teams with talent.

After my sophomore season, a major league team contacted me. They invited my dad and me to discuss signing a contract. It was very difficult for my dad to get off of work, but somehow he found a way to take three consecutive days off from work.

Upon arriving at the team's office, we met with the team's owner and general manager. They told us about the team's interest in signing me, but they did not want to go over the four thousand dollar limit. They mentioned their understanding of my family's financial shortcomings and added another layer to the offer.

"Just because we are not going to give you more than a four

thousand dollar bonus does not mean that we are not prepared to give you additional money," the owner said. "We know you have a large mortgage on your house, and we are prepared to pay it off. We also know you have an older car, and we are prepared to buy you a new one. We know you have other debts and medical expenses, and we are prepared to take care of them as well."

I was very excited because I was going to have the opportunity to pursue my dream and take care of my family. My dad's thoughts on the matter were different.

It did not take my dad more than ten seconds to respond. "Gentlemen, I have always taught my boys and family to do the right thing and live honestly," he said. "We are a Christian family, and we try to live by Christian principles, and that is why we must not entertain your offer. Thank you and good day."

We walked out of their office, and I was shocked. On the way to the airport, I asked him, "Dad, are you sure you know what you are doing?" He reassured me and said there was no doubt in his mind.

For him, it didn't matter that other teams were doing the same thing. It was breaking the rules, and that was enough for him. I thought to myself about how tremendous the financial temptation must have been for my father. I realized the sacrifice he was making for me on so many levels. I never forgot the integrity my father showed that day.

I am forever grateful to him for teaching me that, and I was forever changed.

The following year, 1956, I returned to the University of Minnesota, and we won the College World Series. Following the championship, the Chicago Cubs offered me a signing bonus that met all of my family's needs, and I began my pro career.

I signed the contract with my parents' blessing—with an understanding that I would complete my college education in the offseason.

When I made my debut in the big leagues, my mom and dad were there. They had both helped me get there. And they helped me get there the right way.

My first offseason, the Cubs strongly encouraged me to play winter ball in Cuba to hone my skills. The offer included a generous stipend, a beach house, and the chance to play ball. While the temptation to go was great, I had made a promise to my parents to get a college degree, and I spent the next three winters attending school and staying true to my word and myself.

Just like my dad did that day in the owner's office when he showed me the importance of doing the right thing.

Scout: Vedie Himsl

- AVG .279 • Home Runs 369 • RBIs 1,105
- Pittsburgh Pirates 1946–1953, Chicago Cubs 1953–1954, Cleveland Indians 1955
- Led National League in home runs: 1946–1952
- Led Major League in home runs: 1947–1952
- All-Star: 1948–1953
- Elected to the National Baseball Hall of Fame: 1975

RALPH KINER————•

Adjustments of any kind in life take time to learn, but the
benefit of learning will last a lifetime.

I came into my second spring training as a major league player feeling pretty good.

During my rookie season, I led the league with twenty-three home runs. My team, the Pittsburgh Pirates, had just signed Hank Greenberg to play with us.

Hank was at the end of his career in 1947, and I was just beginning mine. He had already hit more than three hundred home runs, and I was very excited at the thought of having him as a teammate. When I was a kid, I first really became interested in baseball after watching Hank's Detroit Tigers play against the Chicago Cubs in the 1934 World Series. It was an amazing feeling to have as a teammate someone I had idolized as a kid.

I had never met him before our first workout that spring, and I was a little nervous around him. He went about his routine, and I went through mine. We returned to the locker room without speaking and hit the showers and got dressed.

As I was getting dressed, Hank hollered at me, "Hey, kid! Want to stay late and hit some extra batting practice?"

Hank's extra BP sessions had become the stuff of legend. I was honored, and I jumped at the opportunity. As we began the session, he said to me, "Ralph, you realize you'll never hit a lot of home runs the way you are going."

You have to understand that I was a very confident young man who had led the league in homers in my first season in the bigs. If it were anyone other than a hitter I respected as much as Hank, I'm not sure how I would have responded. But I chose to keep my mouth shut and listened to him.

It was probably the smartest decision I ever made as a ballplayer.

"You got my attention last year, kid, because you hit a lot of homers," Hank said. "But pitchers are going to get smarter, and they will expose weaknesses in your stroke. You need to change your approach if you want to keep hitting homers."

He showed me how to change my position in the batter's box to maximize my stroke for power. He told me that if I moved up in the batter's box, I could attack the ball and pull it more.

When we finished that night, he asked me a rhetorical question: "Are you going to be a good hitter or a great hitter? It's really up to you, kid."

I kept my silence again, knowing this was the type of question you answered with your actions and not your words.

The next two months were some of the hardest times of my career. I struggled with my swing, and by Memorial Day weekend, I had only three home runs.

Billy Hermann was our manager, and he was expecting great things from me. He was so disappointed with my production that he told me to go back to my old style or he would send me down to the minors. That's when Hank stepped in. Hank, who was unquestionably our star player, went above Billy to our team owner Frank McKenney and said that if I was sent down, he would quit.

That bought me some time, but I was still struggling with the new approach. I never questioned Hank's advice because I understood what he was telling me, and I believed him. It was just so hard to try something out of my comfort zone. The last day of May, I struck out four times in one game. It was the worst feeling I ever had as a ballplayer.

Hank told me over and over to be patient and remember that adjustments of any kind take time to learn, but the benefits of learning would last a lifetime.

Then, one day it all clicked. All of sudden, I was able to stand at the top of the batter's box and pull the inside pitch for power just like Hank had said I would. Even though I had only three home runs the first two months of the season, I went on a hitting tear and finished with fifty-one home runs.

I had Hank's teaching to thank. And as great a gift as his hitting advice was, the greatest gift I ever received from him was his friendship. He was the best man at my wedding.

How many people can say that about their childhood heroes?

Scout: Hollis "Sloppy" Thurston

- Manager: Chicago White Sox 1979–1986, Oakland Athletics 1986–1995, St. Louis Cardinals 1996–present
- World Series Champion: 1990, 2006

TONY LA RUSSA———•

I found someone whom everyone should try to find in
their own lives.

Toward the end of my professional playing career in 1975, I was given the opportunity to serve as both a player and a coach at the suggestion of Loren Babe, who was managing our farm team.

At the time, my future as a ballplayer was ending. I was eager at the chance to have both roles mainly because, in the short-term, it kept me employed, and my salary could help me pay for my law school tuition.

While I didn't realize it at first, Loren was convinced that I had a future as a manager. Even though I had been a professional baseball player in both the big leagues and minors for more than ten years, I started to really understand the game in a whole new light through Loren's eyes.

Loren would sit with me in the dugout and explain the game as though it were a chess match. I learned quickly that managing was not as simple as filling out a lineup card, and my whole perspective on baseball—and life—soon began to change.

Over two seasons, I was so eager to get to the ballpark and have more conversations with Loren. He would explain everything to me from how to scout a player to defensive strategies to controlling the flow of the game.

I remember one game when all of these lessons and conversations seemed to click for me.

Loren started me at shortstop even though my natural position was second base.

In one of our many conversations, I asked Loren after the game why he played me at short. His response had a profound impact on my understanding the game and the role of a manager when he said, "Because our shortstop was struggling, and the only way to win today was going to be with our offense. Even if I gave up a little defensively with you at shortstop, I gained the benefit of having you bat three times."

It was like a light went off in my head, and my future path was now so very clear to me.

In Loren, I found someone whom everyone should try to find in their own lives. This is simply a trusted friend with a rich background of knowledge and experiences to share that you can talk to without a filter.

Eventually, Loren gave me the chance to manage one inning of an actual game, and I applied his strategies in that first inning and every game I managed in the big leagues ever since.

Scout: Doug Gassaway

- AVG .260 • Hits 2,016 • Home Runs 138
- Pittsburgh Pirates 1956–1972
- Hit a walk-off home run in game seven of the 1960's World Series
- Gold Glove Award: 1958, 1960–1961, 1963–1967
- All-Star: 1958–1960, 1962–1964, 1967
- Elected to the National Baseball Hall of Fame: 2001

BILL MAZEROSKI———•

He believed in me at an age when I really needed it.

At Warren Consolidated High School in Tiltonsville, Ohio, my baseball coach, Al Burazio, was the first one that really talked to me about a future in baseball.

When I was a freshman, he told me I was going to be a big league ballplayer.

Now, this kind of talk seemed far-fetched to me at the time. Even though being a big league ballplayer was all I had ever dreamed about, there was a part of me that never really believed it could happen.

My conversation with Coach somehow made that dream a little more real, and it lit an extra spark inside of me from the moment my high school baseball career began.

Coach stressed fundamentals to me—especially defensive skills. I played shortstop throughout high school, and with Coach's support, scouts from teams like the Yankees, Phillies, and Indians started to talk with me.

However, as he always did, Coach knew best and encouraged me to sign with the Pittsburgh Pirates. Like my high school days, I broke in as a shortstop. I was surprised when I got to my first spring training camp that there were no infield coaches, and we had to learn on our own. It was also quite taboo for the other players to help you too because everyone was so competitive for roster spots.

It was during this time that my life changed forever, and because Coach had stressed fundamentals, I was prepared.

During practice that day, we had seven shortstops and no one to play second base. The Pirates coaches gave me the opportunity to play second base that day, and I stayed there for the rest of my career.

Looking back, I realized how much I needed Coach's influence in my life in two ways. First, he believed in me at an age when I really needed it, and secondly, the lessons he gave me prepared me for the moment when my destiny appeared.

Without his coaching, both on and off the field, I'm not sure I would have been able to be ready for that moment when I played second base for the very first time.

I played second base for seventeen seasons and won seven Gold

Gloves as a reward for my defensive abilities.

After I retired, I was able to properly thank Coach for all his influence on me.

It is still amazing to me to this day to think that everything he predicted would happen has come true.

Scout: Rex Bowen

• ─────────────────────────CAREER HIGHLIGHTS

- AVG .306 • Home Runs 234 • Hits 3,319
- Milwaukee Brewers 1978–1992, Toronto Blue Jays 1993–1995, Minnesota Twins 1996–1998
- All-Star: 1980, 1985, 1988, 1991–1994
- World Series Champion: 1993
- World Series MVP: 1993
- Elected to the National Baseball Hall of Fame: 2004

PAUL MOLITOR———————•

Reaching your dreams is a process that is built over time.

In 1987, I was entering my ninth year in the majors. I had endured a lot of injuries, and I had been on the disabled list about twenty times.

I didn't realize it then, but what I was really in need of was advice. I was ready to hear some positive guidance because I had been labeled as injury prone, and some part of me was starting to believe it. I knew I had done okay as a hitter when I was healthy, but as I was about to learn, being okay was not good enough.

One day around the All-Star break that year, our hitting coach, Tony Muser, asked, "Paul, what level do you think you can compete at in the majors?"

I was not sure where he was going with this, but I told him my goal was to be a .300 hitter. I had eclipsed .300 three times already in my career and felt this was the level every hitter should aim for.

He looked at me, almost like a disappointed father, and said, "If you hit .300 in the big leagues, you are obviously a pretty good hitter. But you are better than that. You need to take off your own limitations. You need to set higher goals for yourself because you have the potential to be great. You can't be afraid to raise the bar." He continued by saying, "Ask any of your teammates their goals at the start of the season, and if they say to hit .260 and hit twenty home runs, then that is what they will likely do. If you want great things to happen, you have to get out of your comfort zone and extend yourself more in your mind."

I'm not even sure if I responded to him, but I know I soaked it all in. After the All-Star break, armed with Tony's insights, I went on a thirty-nine game hitting streak. I started to believe more in myself and no longer settled with mediocre or even good performances.

In the ensuing years, I hit .353, .340, and .320—which were significantly higher than my previous best seasons—and Tony's advice continued to propel me to accomplish more.

Life to me became all about goal setting.

Reaching your dreams is a process that is built over time. Tony taught me the power to shoot for great dreams and to be open to working hard for them. It freed my mind to do better in the short term and allowed me to raise expectations in the long run.

Scouts: Dee Fondy and Emil Belich

- Wins 230 • ERA 4.21 • Strikeouts 2,125
- Chicago Cubs 1986–1988, Texas Rangers 1989–1990, St. Louis Cardinals 1991, Baltimore Orioles 1993–1995, Boston Red Sox 1996, Seattle Mariners 1996–2006, Philadelphia Phillies 2006–2007
- Roberto Clemente Award: 2003
- All-Star: 2003

JAMIE MOYER——————•

Why change who you are to be successful?

The Chicago Cubs drafted me in the sixth round of the 1984 amateur draft.

This was a great surprise to me because I was told I was not going to get drafted until the fifteenth round.

Little did I know that this would be the first of many surprises in my career.

The Cubs sent me right to their New York-Penn League team, and within two years I made my big league debut.

I was 7-4 my first year in the majors, and in 1987, my first full season, I finished with a record just under .500. My record kept dropping below .500 until the Cubs traded me before the 1989 season to the Texas Rangers. My sub-.500 performances continued, and the Rangers released me.

Luckily, the St. Louis Cardinals signed me to a one-year deal for the 1991 season. I started the season in Class AAA Louisville and played some with the Cardinals too. I didn't win a game that entire season at the big league level.

It was the longest summer of my life.

My wife and I had just started a family, and I was very worried about the future.

The Cubs offered me a coaching job, but I still had a burning desire to compete on the field, not from the bench. I turned down the coaching job and went home and just worked out a ton that offseason.

The Detroit Tigers offered me a spot to pitch with the Class AAA Toledo team in 1992, and I spent the summer in the minors. Before I knew it, I was a free agent again.

I was now six years into my career and had a losing record and been released or traded by four clubs. My prospects were not good, but I still believed in my ability to get big league hitters out.

I was at a crossroads in my life.

I remember feeling that I believed in myself with the Cubs, but I was still very green. I moved quickly through the ranks, but I was so green when I got to the majors and just couldn't perform well at the big league level. We were starting a family, and I didn't have a team that wanted me. The facts were simple: no one was interested in signing a thirty-year-old career sub-.500 pitcher.

That is until another surprise happened.

This surprise was Henry Dorfman coming into my life. He was a great baseball man, but not in the way that most great baseball men are. Henry was a master at the mental side of the game.

I spent three days with him that offseason and just talked about baseball and life. I spilled my guts out to him. Through talking to him, I realized I needed more confidence in my ability and was not comfortable in my own shoes as a pitcher or content with who I was.

Learning that lesson was as valuable as anything I ever learned mechanically because I was successful in the minors, but I couldn't figure out why I was struggling at the major league level.

My failures at the big league level all had to do with confidence. I was scared. I was not myself at the major league level because I did not believe deep down inside that I could get those guys out in the same way that I believed I could at the minor league level.

"Why change who you are to be successful?" he asked me.

I did not have to answer him because the question itself was the answer I was seeking.

From that moment on, I had an unwavering belief in being myself. A renewed commitment to myself and my craft was almost born naturally out of this realization.

It was about this time that the phone rang, and it was Baltimore Orioles general manager Roland Hemond. He offered me a spot on their team, and he said he believed in me, and if I did not make the big league club, he would save a spot on the team's Class AAA Rochester team.

With my newfound approach, I made the team and felt like I was on my way and better than ever. By May, I had lost my first three games, but I did not doubt myself or my approach, and almost overnight, I went on a tear.

I won five games in a row!

Now I went from doubting myself at the big league level and

thinking about quitting to a renewed desire to get back to prove my abilities to no one else but me. I was truthful to myself for the first time in my life and looked in the mirror and saw myself not just for what I wanted to be but what I really was: good and bad. There was a tremendous strength to this both as a pitcher and as man. It was one of the toughest lessons I have learned but also the most valuable to be able to see myself rationally.

After that season with the Orioles, I never looked at the pitcher's mound as the stage of the highest level or as pressure, but with a renewed calmness and focus.

Before meeting Henry, I would give up a hit and think to myself and panic all there by myself on the mound and say, "Here I go again!" I would become stressed, and that feeling would snowball to the point where I was not able to perform at my best.

Then I learned to not worry about it and be positive. As simple as it sounds, it really worked for me. I directed energies in life in ways I could benefit from, and the more positive I was with my energies and beliefs, the more ways I could succeed.

From that moment on, I was playing on borrowed time. I think that was the key to allowing me to receive the biggest surprise of my career: the chance to compete as a major league pitcher until my mid forties.

Scout: Billy Blitzer

- Wins 318 • ERA 3.35 • Strikeouts 3,342
- Milwaukee/Atlanta Braves 1964–1983, 1987, New York Yankees 1984–1985, Cleveland Indians 1986–1987, Toronto Blue Jays 1987
- Most innings pitched by any pitcher in the live-ball era ($5,404^{1/3}$)
- All-Star: 1969, 1975, 1978, 1982, 1984
- Gold Glove Award: 1978–1980, 1982–1983
- Elected to the National Baseball Hall of Fame: 1997

PHIL NIEKRO————————.

I thought about my dad every single time I buttoned up my Major League Baseball jersey.

Growing up in Lansing, Ohio, my brother, Joe, and I would sit on the back porch every day with our mitts, waiting for our dad to come back from the coal mines to play ball with us.

Dad would come home from work with his lunch pail and sneak us an extra Twinkie, and then we'd have a catch until dinner and listen to Cleveland Indians games on the radio. Dad would fall asleep and somehow have enough energy to get up before sunrise and go to work and do it all over again.

It was in the backyard that I picked up the knuckleball. At the time I didn't really know what a knuckleball was—all I knew was I could get people out with it. So when I went to tryout camp as an eighteen-year-old, I got signed by the Milwaukee Braves for a five hundred dollar bonus and a salary of two hundred and seventy-five dollars a month.

That was 1957, and by 1959 I was pitching in the big leagues.

I couldn't throw hard, but I didn't let it stop me. I wasn't even the athlete in my family. That title belonged to my brother, Joe.

Once I signed and started playing in the minors, I stopped and thought how fortunate I was to be paid to play baseball. I remembered my dad's words about work, "Make sure you earn your dollar every day."

He worked in the coal mines his whole life, and I learned the value of work just by watching him. His inspiration and love drove me to succeed in baseball because I didn't want to work in the coal mines. Dad was a great player in his day. He played semipro, and he could have been a pro player had life worked out differently for him.

Joe and I decided that when we made it to the big leagues, we would wear the major league uniform for him. I thought about my dad in the locker room every single time I buttoned up that major league jersey.

It was family pride that pushed me as much as anything physically. And it was family pride that taught me never to take anything for granted.

Scout: Bill Maughn

- Career Batting Average .288
- 1937, O'Neil signed with the Memphis Red Sox for their first year of play in the newly-formed Negro American League
- Played in four East-West All-Star games and two Negro League World Series
- O'Neil took over as player/manager of the Kansas City Monarchs and guided them to two league titles in 1953 and 1955
- Named the first black coach in the major leagues by the Chicago Cubs in 1962

BUCK O'NEIL————————•

There is something better, but you can't get it here. You are going to have to go someplace else.

When I was very young, I was working as a box boy in the celery fields near our home in Sarasota, Florida. I got the job from my daddy, who was also my boss. It was my job to put the boxes out for the farmers to pack celery in before shipping them. It was not necessarily hard work, but it was very repetitive and incredibly hot. One day, I was sitting behind the boxes I had stacked up, sweating, and I just sat down for a moment.

I just kind of muttered out loud to myself, "*Damn.* It's so hot. There's gotta to be something better out there for me than this." I kinda dreamed off for a second and then returned to work and didn't think about it again until the ride home when my daddy brought it up. He said he was on the other side of the boxes and heard what I said.

At first I thought I was in trouble because I said damn. But then he said, "I got the job from my dad, who was also my boss. I heard what you said about there being something better than this. There is something better, but you can't get it here. You're gonna have to go someplace else."

That someplace else turned out not to be a place but a game: baseball.

My uncle worked for a railroad company, and he came to visit us in Sarasota. During this visit, he took my daddy and me to the Poinciana Hotel in West Palm Beach to see the great Rube Foster, the President of the Negro Leagues.

Now, I had seen the major leagues, but this type of baseball was different. It was faster and seemed so exciting to me that I knew I had found my "someplace else." When I got back home, I was a chatterbox and talked to everyone I could meet about how exciting it was. I think my daddy picked up on my enthusiasm, and we talked at length about it. We followed the players in newspapers, and I practiced every day.

That experience meant everything to me as a young boy. It still does today. That moment meant so much to me that it is still hard to put into words. It meant my getting out of that celery field. It meant improving my life, my children's lives. From that moment on, I no longer had to spend energy wondering if there was something better out there for me. Instead, the energy was spent working at becoming a ballplayer because my destiny became apparent to me.

And just about ten years later, my days as a celery box boy were over, and I was being paid to play professional baseball.

- AVG .279 • Home Runs 379 • Hits 2,732
- Cincinnati Reds 1964–1976, 1984–1986, Montreal Expos 1977–1979, Boston Red Sox 1980–1982, Philadelphia Phillies 1983
- All-Star: 1967–1970, 1974–1976
- All-Star MVP: 1967
- World Series Champion: 1975, 1976
- Elected to the National Baseball Hall of Fame: 2000

T O N Y   P E R E Z

I never doubted myself and stayed positive through it all,
and I believe this was a key to my long career.

When I was a very young boy, I did not play much baseball because I was working all of the time with my dad in the sugar business. There were six of us in my family, and we all had to work together to make enough money to live.

My father always supported me in anything I did, and he loved baseball as much as I did. I knew at a very young age that I wanted to be a baseball player. I didn't like working at the factory, and I didn't want that for my life, so I wanted to be a baseball player.

When I signed my first professional baseball contract, I remember thinking this was my chance, and I didn't want to let myself or my family down. It was at this time that Fidel Castro took over Cuba, and my father never said stay there. He told me, "Tony, go to America and do the best you can. If you help us, great, but do your best and always keep a positive attitude."

I knew I wanted to be somebody, and I saw my best opportunity to do that as a baseball player. My chance to finally be somebody came on July 26, 1964, when the Cincinnati Reds called me up to the big leagues for the first time.

After I received a call from the Reds, I heard from Tony Pacheco, the scout that signed me to my first professional contract.

"Congratulations on making the Reds, but try not to get too excited because making it to the big leagues is one thing. Staying there is another challenge," he told me. "Do not put too much pressure on yourself and just do your best. One of the toughest things to do is not to look back or compare yourself to other ballplayers."

With Tony's words and my dad's influence on keeping a positive attitude, I headed to the big leagues looking ahead to the future and determined to stay there.

I was learning to play the game in another language, and that was hard, but in my mind, it was just another obstacle. I learned how to communicate, and it became easier. I ended up learning more and concentrating more because of the language barrier.

My positive attitude helped me not to be frustrated with the language problems, and I never got down on myself or believed in slumps. My attitude was that good pitching was getting me out. I always believed that if I didn't do my best, the pitching was just good.

I was very positive all the time and gave credit to the pitchers because I knew they were trying their best to beat me. I would say to myself, "It's not a slump." I never doubted myself and stayed positive through it all, and I believe this was a key to my long career. It just was not worth it to get down on myself.

This helped me to stay positive and work at competing at this level without putting too much pressure on myself. To me, pressure is not hitting a baseball. Pressure is my dad and my family working long hours just to put food on the table.

Looking back, I know those early days working with my dad helped me to stay positive and work hard no matter what I faced on the baseball field.

Scout: Tony Pacheco

- Wins 314 • ERA 3.11 • Strikeouts 3,534
- San Francisco Giants 1962–1971, Cleveland Indians 1972–1975, Texas Rangers 1975–1977, 1980, San Diego Padres 1978–1979, New York Yankees 1980, Atlanta Braves 1981, Seattle Mariners 1982–1983, Kansas City Royals 1983
- All-Star: 1966, 1970, 1972, 1974, 1979
- Cy Young Award: 1972, 1978
- Elected to the National Baseball Hall of Fame: 1991

GAYLORD PERRY⸺⸺•

I promised myself that this time I was here to stay.

When I reached the major leagues in 1962, I figured it meant that I was also pitching in my last minor league game.

Boy, was I wrong.

The next two years it felt like I was playing on two teams because I was always shuffling between the San Francisco Giants and our minor league club.

As I got impatient during this time, my pitching coach told me that my time would come and said, "Don't worry about things you can't control. You can control how you prepare and whether you are physically and mentally ready. Your opportunity will come, but until it does, do not worry about it. Just worry about what you can control."

I tried to follow his advice, but all the back and forth was difficult, especially because I believed in my abilities to get big league hitters out.

Then, in May of 1964, my prophecy came true in the most unlikely of ways. I promised myself that this time I was here to stay in the majors. Now, please understand every ballplayer makes this promise to himself, but this time it really happened because I had an opportunity—and I was prepared.

That moment came in the most unexpected of situations on May 31, 1964. It was the second game of a doubleheader against the Mets in Shea Stadium.

I was sitting in the bullpen, and we were in extra innings in the second game. By this time I got to know the security guard very well because there was no one left in the pen but me. In the twelfth inning, I was told to start warming up. I was so excited to get into the game that I didn't even wait for them to send a catcher from the dugout. I tossed a glove to the security guard and started warming up with him until the catcher arrived.

I took over in the bottom of the thirteenth. My catcher, Tom Haller, told me to really barrel down and go for it. I followed Tom's wisdom and went for it with all I had on every pitch. I pitched ten shutout innings, and the game ended in the twenty-third inning. It lasted a record seven hours and twenty-three minutes. Not only did I get the win, but I also earned the respect of my teammates and most importantly my manager, Alvin Dark, whom I knew would not send me down again after that performance.

Scouts: Earl Smith, Tim Murchison, and Tom Sheehan

- Pittsburgh Pirates 1951–1953
- Appeared in twelve major league games
- Fourteen career strikeouts
- Nicknamed the "Bonus Baby" for signing baseball's first six-figure bonus contract as a high school star

PAUL PETTIT————————•

I could no longer throw a baseball. It was just too painful to pitch.

My story starts with the constant advice of my recreation director, Lyn Isch, while I was growing up. He was the playground director, and he starting emphasizing to us at a very early age the importance of an education. Looking back, his constant reinforcement of a college degree had a profound impact on me even though I didn't realize it at the time.

You have to understand that I had a wonderfully successful amateur career at Narbonne High in Lomita, Calif. I once struck out twenty seven batters in a twelve inning game and pitched six no-hitters.

This success helped catapult me to become baseball's first six-figure bonus player. At the age of eighteen in 1951, I signed a then-record one hundred thousand dollar contract with the Pittsburgh Pirates, and my future seemed so bright. I was christened the "Bonus Baby" by the media and thrust into the limelight, and a trail of publicity followed my every step. It seemed like every day there was an article about my every move.

If you would have asked anyone at the time, it would seem the best move I ever made was signing that contract, but in reality, it was starting college simultaneously with my professional baseball career. I enrolled in college and took classes on a part-time basis.

At the time, it seemed rather cliché, but there is a beauty in understanding that no one could take away your education.

This was an important lesson for me because baseball was taken away from me. I made my major league debut at nineteen years old, but I had a rude awakening. I had a bad arm and worked at rehabilitating my injury in 1952. In 1953, I was back with the Pirates and had my first start and thought everything would be rosy, but by spring training in 1954, I could no longer throw a baseball. It was just too painful to pitch.

I tried to play other positions and had some decent years in the minor leagues and came close as a position player, but I never reached the majors again.

You can't imagine the frustration I felt because I was still so young, and all the publicity surrounding my signing made it tough, but at such a young age, I had to now rethink, a new plan for my future.

Baseball, like a lot of things in life, can be very unstable, and education provides the ultimate stability. I pursued my baseball career with passion, and it was my dream. That was my Plan A, but life requires a Plan B, and education is as stable of a Plan B as there is out there. I am forever grateful to Lyn for not only saying the words but for insisting that I take that cliché and turn it into a reality.

It was the best decision I ever made in my life.

By the time I was thirty, I had earned my bachelor's degree and began my life as a teacher, and I'm most proud that all of my children and grandchildren have all earned college degrees as well.

Scouts: Tom Downey and Roy Hamey

- Wins 211 • ERA 3.27 • Strikeouts 1,999
- Detroit Tigers 1945, 1948, Chicago White Sox 1949–1961, San Francisco Giants 1962–1964
- Won fifteen or more games eight times
- All-Star: 1953, 1955–59, 1961
- Led American League in strikeouts: 1953
- Led American League in ERA: 1955

BILL PIERCE ——————•

A positive attitude will quickly turn the bad into good, and it can create a new path to greater destiny, as I did with my curveball.

My father was a pharmacist. As much as I loved sports, I had always planned on becoming a doctor. Baseball was just kind of a thing I did as a child, like a lot of other sports I was playing at the time.

In my junior year of high school, my coach, Ray Stites, came to my dad's drug store, looked me square in the eye, and said, "Bill, you have a position on the football team, but I would advise you to stick to baseball. You have a gift, and you have the potential to make it if you are willing to work at it and not get distracted by any obstacles." This was the first moment that I realized that I had a future in baseball, because someone who understood talent and the game told me so. My parents had always supported me unconditionally and told me I could do anything I set my mind to, but this was something different. Amazingly enough, within two years of that conversation, I was the starting pitcher for the Detroit Tigers at the age of eighteen years old.

The next turning point for me, however, did not happen for another eight years, in 1953.

By this time, I had been traded to the Chicago White Sox and had matured into a solid starting pitcher, throwing 250-plus innings for several years in a row and winning about twelve to fifteen games a year.

One day, I was in the backyard throwing the football around with my family, and I felt a pinch and a pain I had never felt before.

When I got back to spring training that year, I could not throw over my shoulder. It was just too painful. I wondered how I was going to take care of my young family. I considered ending my big league dreams and returning home and working as a doctor back at the pharmacy. It was at this moment that for some reason, I remembered that conversation with Coach Stites and how much he believed in me.

I decided I would not quit and would find a way to get through this terrible pain. I talked to our trainer Eddie Froelich about the pain. He developed a very simple method for me to take two aspirin before every game, and he routinely rubbed my shoulder with a hot rub. I learned to pitch through the pain. After twenty minutes, the pain subsided enough for me to pitch.

I did this before every start the rest of my career, and it opened up a deeper level of commitment for me.

While the pain was substantial and a major physical obstacle, I never let it get to me to mentally or emotionally. And like many experiences in life, there was a silver lining to be found in the pain.

My pitching coach, Ray Berry, helped me to understand that this freak injury changed my pitching motion. It also ultimately led me to throw a more effective curveball that became my hallmark pitch.

In 1955, pitching with the pain, I led the majors with an earned run average of 1.97, and the two following seasons, I had back-to-back twenty-win seasons—thanks largely to the new, more effective curveball.

I learned during this time that baseball, like life, is designed to give you good and bad streaks. The key is when you get hurt or are thrown a bad streak to persevere and understand how to embrace the change, always stay positive, and listen to those around you who care about you and let them help. A positive attitude will quickly turn the bad into good, and it can create a new path to greater destiny—like it did with my curveball.

No matter what dream anyone pursues in life, there will be obstacles, and you have to be dedicated to find a way to succeed and persevere with what resources are available to you. A lot of guys back then were injured and never returned to pitch again. Physical therapy and rotator cuff surgery did not exist in the 1950s, and it would have been easy to quit, but I never stopped believing in myself.

I don't think I would have ever imagined it when I was injured that day in the backyard, but the confidence that Coach Stites had in me inspired me twice in life, and that injury helped me to realize my potential as a pitcher.

Scouts: Lou D'Annunzio and Wish Egan

CAREER HIGHLIGHTS

- AVG .318 • Hits 2,304 • Home Runs 207
- Minnesota Twins 1984–1995
- Gold Glove Award: 1986–1989, 1991, 1992
- Silver Slugger Award: 1986–1989, 1992, 1994
- All-Star: 1986–1995
- Led the American League in batting average: 1989
- Elected to the National Baseball Hall of Fame: 2001

KIRBY PUCKETT————•

The key to unlocking your true power and strength is to
never be afraid to fail.

I was sitting in a hotel room in Old Orchard, Maine, with my minor league teammate Tack Wilson when our manager, Cal Ermer, walked in.

"Congratulations kid," Cal said. "You are going to the show."

I thought he was talking to Tack, but Cal said he meant me. I could not believe it. I was finally going to be a major league player.

I packed my bags as quickly as I could and headed to the airport for the long flight to Anaheim, with a layover in Atlanta. When I arrived in California, I went straight to the stadium to join my teammates for a game against the California Angels. Because it had been such a long trip, I was told that I would not be playing that night, but the next night I would be the starting centerfielder for the Minnesota Twins.

I was the youngest of nine children, so I had lots of friends and family to tell the great news. I think I called all of them from California to share the excitement of my boyhood dream coming true.

When I was called up, I was nervous, but I was never afraid. As I was growing up and playing pickup games against older kids or my brothers or at Calumet High School in Chicago, my father repeatedly told me to never be afraid to fail. He told me over and over again that if you have not failed, you have not lived. I was beginning to understand his words right then and there, living as a major league player.

The next day, I was the Twins' starting center fielder and leadoff hitter. Since we were the visiting team, I was the first batter of the game. All of the adrenaline helped me to hit the ball hard, but it was fielded by Angels infielder Dick Schofield, and he threw me out by a step. I remember thinking as I trotted back to the dugout that the ball would have been a hit in the minor leagues.

As I found a seat in the dugout, I thought about being thrown out, and my thoughts turned to my father.

My dad had passed away a few years before, when I was in college. Now, I was picturing him telling me what he told me all the time as a young boy, "Never be afraid to fail, Kirby. Everyone fails. Everyone. You can't worry about things you can't control. The key to unlocking your true power and strength is to never be afraid to fail."

There I was, sitting in a major league dugout, but in my mind, I was little Kirby Puckett again. And my father was sharing with me wisdom that made so much sense in the moment after my first big league at-bat.

I was initially frustrated because I knew I would only have one first at-bat in the majors, and I was disappointed that I did not get a hit. So I focused on learning from that at-bat. I could not control that Dick and the rest of the Angels were better than the players I had faced in the minors. I had to go up to the plate unafraid the next time and focus on what I could control: my ability to hit the ball.

In my next at-bat, I got my first big league hit. I stole second and scored a run. I ended up going four-for-five that day. My father's fearless attitude was in me. From that moment on, I approached the game, and my life, unafraid to fail.

Like every ballplayer and every human being, I failed lots of times throughout my career. But because of my father's words, I understood the power of learning from failure. It was his words, as much as any ability I had on the baseball field, that helped me learn to succeed many times in my career and in my life.

Scout: Ellsworth Brown

- AVG .294 • Home Runs 586 • RBIs 1,812
- Cincinnati Reds 1956–1965, Baltimore Orioles 1966–1971, Los Angeles Dodgers 1972, California Angels 1973–1974, Cleveland Indians 1974–1976
- All-Star: 1956–1957, 1959, 1961–1962, 1965–1967, 1969–1971, 1974
- MVP: 1961, 1966
- American League Triple Crown: 1966
- World Series MVP: 1966
- Elected to the National Baseball Hall of Fame: 1982

F R A N K   R O B I N S O N⎯⎯⎯•

Those words drove me ... to be the best person I could be and appreciate every gift I have and everyone I encounter.

When I was about ten years old, I played all kinds of sports with my friends in the neighborhood. It did not matter what we were playing. About this time, I started to realize that I had a gift for playing sports.

While I was doing well in the neighborhood games, I never gave much thought to making a career out of it; I just liked playing sports.

Besides, this was in the mid-1940s, and African Americans were not allowed to play in the big leagues until 1947. Up until Jackie Robinson entered the majors in 1947, I was always "playing" sports. Once it became a reality that I would have the opportunity to play in the major leagues, I thought I had a realistic chance to make a living from baseball.

I must have told a lot of people this because it was about this time that my mother made sure that no matter what I pursued in life that I would be humble. She wouldn't let me feel special, and she told me words that stuck with me my entire life, "Just remember that you are no better than anyone else in this world because you have a God-given gift to hit a baseball."

Those words drove me as a young boy, a ballplayer, and later as a manager to be the best person I could be and appreciate every gift I have and everyone I encounter.

My mom's words mean the same to me today as it did then, but I understand it more now with reflection.

As a young boy, it taught me to be a great teammate.

As a professional player, it showed me how to be respectful to opponents.

As a manager, it taught me to teach the fundamentals so players could apply them to their God-given talents.

I was able to become a manager, I believe, because of my mom's wisdom as much as anything else I ever did in the game.

Scout: Bobby Mattick

- Wins 324 • Strikeouts 5,714 • ERA 3.19
- New York Mets 1966, 1968–1971, California Angels 1972–1979, Houston Astros 1980–1988, Texas Rangers 1989–1993
- MLB-record seven career no-hitters
- All-Star: 1972–1973, 1975, 1977, 1979, 1981, 1985, 1989
- Elected to the National Baseball Hall of Fame: 1999

N O L A N   R Y A N———————•

There are no shortcuts with work.

Everyone has mentors and people that had influence in their lives. The key, at least for me, is to not only recognize them but to learn from them.

My earliest mentors were my parents.

I started playing in the big leagues for the New York Mets when I was nineteen years old. I was too young and naïve to realize at the time how much influence my parents had on me, especially their work ethic.

Throughout my childhood, my dad worked two jobs. He had one at the petroleum company, and he also distributed the *Houston Post*. His dedication to his family and approach to both jobs was the reason I and my siblings had better opportunities for our own lives.

Besides just learning from his example, I'd have odd summer jobs like painting houses and mowing lawns to earn pocket money. Little did I realize that I was also learning valuable lessons that would help me in my baseball career.

A few times, I'd cut corners while mowing lawns so I could get done sooner to go meet my friends. My dad always seemed to know when I would do this, and he would go check on my work.

"There are no shortcuts with work," he told me, and then he would have me do the entire lawn over again to reinforce the lesson.

His words and these experiences had a profound impact on my life and on my career because it taught me never to cut corners.

The realities of making the big leagues at such an early age is both a blessing and a curse. I realize now I was physically ready for the challenge, but my mental game was as young as my teenage years. I did not really approach baseball as a career as much. My mindset was simply that I was just thrilled to be paid to be a ballplayer.

Thankfully, at this time in my life, I had Tom Seaver as a teammate.

Even though I started on the Mets before him, Tom was a few years older and definitely had wiser approaches to life than I did.

Tom's greatest impression on me was how disciplined he was with his goal setting. I remember having a conversation with him one day when he told me that his first goal was to pitch in the big leagues for ten years.

This was one of those comments that could have gone in one ear and out the other, but for some reason it stayed with me.

In the weeks that followed, I saw how dedicated Tom was, and that had a huge impact on me because it made me want to take the same approach to my career. Before this moment, I was just happy to be a ballplayer and honestly never gave much thought to the future.

This was not one of those overnight moments. It really kick-started a process of thoughts that showed me what I could be over time. What a rare opportunity I had to be a big league pitcher. I was blessed with a great arm and the opportunity to have a long and successful career.

This moment helped me to focus and set goals of my own and look at baseball as a career.

And because of my parents work ethic and Tom's influence, I ended up with a twenty-seven year big league career that exceeded all of my nineteen-year-old self's wildest dreams.

Scout: John "Red" Murff

- AVG .285 • Home Runs 282 • Hits 2,386
- Philadelphia Phillies 1981, Chicago Cubs 1982–1994, 1996–1997
- Gold Glove Award: 1983–1991
- The Sporting News Player of the Year: 1984
- National League MVP: 1984
- Silver Slugger Award: 1984, 1985, 1988–1992
- All-Star: 1984–1993
- Elected to the National Baseball Hall of Fame: 2005

RYNE SANDBERG———•

By stepping out of my comfort zone and trying something
new, my destiny was forever changed.

In spring training of 1984, I was entering my third season in the big leagues. The Cubs had just hired Jim Frey as our new manager. I knew Jim had a great reputation of being a hitter's coach from stories I heard about him working with George Brett and Darryl Strawberry.

The first week in spring training he did not say much to me. He just watched me hit. I had pretty good foot speed, so I was always taught to try to slap the ball on the ground and run as hard as I could to get on base.

After two weeks of watching me slap the ball around and running hard to first base, he finally talked to me and said, "Ryno, I'm watching you play, and I want you to know that I want you out there every day to be our second baseman. It looks like you are running so hard to first base that I'm worried you're going to pull a hamstring sooner or later. Wouldn't it be nice every once in awhile if you could jog around the bases after a home run?"

I nodded and replied with a question, "Who's going to hit the home runs?"

He smiled at me and said, "You, kid! Meet me at the cages at 8:00 a.m., and we'll do some drills."

The next morning he had me exaggerate my swing to pull the baseball about thirty feet outside the foul line. The goal was to hit the ball into the first few rows of the seats.

That was the start of a whole new future for me.

As with anything that is new in life, it felt very uncomfortable for me, but I was willing to try it because I could see how much Jim believed in what he was teaching me. I also knew that I really struggled on inside pitches because I could not slap those for hits, and this was a way to overcome a weakness of mine.

It's very hard in life to change and do something that doesn't feel right. Life, I've now learned, is all about adjustments if you want to get better. I really felt that this was an adjustment, and no matter how uncomfortable it felt, I knew it would make me better.

We had a game that day, and Jim told me to listen for a whistle. If I heard a whistle, it meant Jim thinks a fastball is coming and to use the pull swing and try to drive the ball.

Even though it still felt weird, I had some immediate success with it. I started hitting the ball harder and could notice a difference in the result.

My first two years in the big leagues, pitchers could get me out all the time with inside fastballs. Now, for the first time, even though it was still spring training, I was not only making contact on those pitches but driving them for extra base hits and home runs.

We started the season in 1984 on the West Coast against the Giants, and I hit my one and only career opening day home run. It was against their closer, Greg Minton, who had a very good sinking fastball that he would throw inside against righties. It was the kind of pitch that used to get me out.

Now, I drove it out of the park in a real game.

It was during this time that I realized that Jim was changing my destiny, and he, like all great mentors, expected more out of me than I thought of myself. I had the talent, but this simple mindset was bringing out an entirely new level of potential in me.

All of these realizations came together for me when that potential became reality on June 23, 1984. We were playing the St. Louis Cardinals in a nationally televised game. I was set to face Bruce Sutter, who was the top relief pitcher in the game. His out pitch was a split-finger fastball that was exactly the type of pitch that I struggled with just a few months ago.

However, armed with my new approach and confidence, I drove two of those pitches from Sutter over the left field fence at Wrigley Field and ended the day five for six with two homers and seven RBIs.

I was winning games for the team in the clutch by driving the type of pitch that I usually missed. I was almost numb at first, but it was such a wonderful feeling for myself. Most importantly, the win put us one game out in the National League Eastern Division, and it propelled us to a division championship that was the first playoff appearance for the Cubs in almost forty years. I was honored with the league's Most Valuable Player award.

And it all started, in my mind, with Jim's advice that day. By stepping out of my comfort zone and trying something new, my destiny was forever changed, and that is a path for anyone to consider.

Scout: Bill Harper

- AVG .277 • Home Runs 342 • RBIs 1,331
- Chicago Cubs 1960–1973, Chicago White Sox 1974
- All-Star: 1963–1966, 1968–1969, 1971–1973
- Gold Glove Award: 1964–1968
- Lou Gehrig Memorial Award: 1973

RON SANTO

My dream of being a big leaguer was worth more than any signature.

My parents were already divorced by the time I was five years old. My dad was a merchant marine, and I don't really have many memories of him. His biggest problem was that he was an alcoholic.

During the time they were getting divorced, my dad came into my room at four in the morning. He woke me up and handed me a baseball.

He told me, "Keep this ball safe. Don't use it. It is your future." He then disappeared as he always seemed to do, and I didn't see him for a long time.

I did what he told me to do and put the ball up on the mantle. I didn't use it, but I would look at that baseball a lot. At night, I would sometimes sleep with that baseball—the same way other children might sleep with a teddy bear.

One day we were playing baseball in the neighborhood, and the ball we were using was hit into the woods, and we lost it. We were so poor that we would often use balls of tape as our baseballs, but I had another idea. I hadn't seen my dad in seven years, and I cared more about that game at that moment, so I ran back into the house, and grabbed the ball that dad had given me. We used that one for a while until someone hit it into the woods and we lost it.

That's the kind of neighborhood I grew up in. We just played ball all the time, and we did everything we could to find players or balls to keep the games going.

I had started playing Little League Baseball at age seven. I snuck into the league because it was supposed to be for eight-year-olds, but I already had a burning desire to play baseball.

When I was twelve, I snuck my way into a Pony League for kids thirteen and up. In two more years, I was playing American Legion ball. It was a theme for me. Because I was always the youngest player on the team, I was not as developed physically as the other players, so it forced me to play a little harder.

This pattern continued until I was a freshman in high school, because freshmen were not allowed to play varsity ball. But when the varsity third baseman got hurt, they made an exception for me, and I got called up as a freshman.

When I was called up, our sophomore shortstop Tim Smith was the best player on our team. He could run, hit, throw, and field. He could do it all, and I thought he would be a big league player. I worked so hard to emulate him.

By the time I was a sophomore, I felt my abilities had caught up to his. When he was a senior, he kind of leveled off, and I kept developing. At one point, I had sixteen major league scouts interested in me.

When someone I admired as much as Tim did not make it, I started to wonder about my chances. The scouts told me that I had not reached my peak yet, and I knew that I had a real chance to make it.

After Tim graduated, I didn't have anyone to drive me, but those words the scouts said to me still did. I kept working hard, and when I graduated, the scouts officially began offering contracts.

I signed with the Chicago Cubs.

Shortly after, as I was getting closer to my dream, I saw my dad again for the first time in about fifteen years. He asked me where that ball was, and I told him what had happened to it. He told me the ball was very valuable—Babe Ruth, Lou Gehrig, and some of their Yankees teammates had signed it.

It was valuable, I thought, but to me, it was valuable in a different way. That ball opened the door for me to a love of baseball. My dream of being a big leaguer was worth more than any signature.

Scout: Dave Kosher

- AVG .267 • Home Runs 548 • RBIs 1,595
- Philadelphia Phillies 1972–1989
- All-Star: 1974, 1976–1977, 1979–1984, 1986–1987, 1989
- Gold Glove Awards: 1976–1984, 1986
- Silver Slugger Award: 1980–1984, 1986
- National League MVP: 1980–1981, 1986
- World Series Champion: 1980
- Elected to the National Baseball Hall of Fame: 1995

MIKE SCHMIDT———•

Just see what happens.

In 1967, I graduated from high school in Dayton, Ohio, and headed to Ohio University. I decided on Ohio primarily because of its reputation as one of the best colleges for architecture. It also had the best baseball program around, and I figured I'd also try out for the baseball team.

Little did I know that I would build a career in baseball instead of buildings.

I had played on my high school team, but I was not a big prospect. I was never offered a scholarship. I never even made all-city or all-state. But Bob Wren, Ohio's coach, saw something in me during tryouts, and I made the team as a walk-on.

My first year, I hit .260 as a switch-hitting shortstop. I was a back-up to Rich McKinney. Then, my whole life changed when Rich signed a pro contract. That opened the door for a starting job for me.

I had become a switch-hitter back in high school because I was tired of being afraid of the ball. I went four-for-four the first time I hit left-handed, and I thought I should continue switch-hitting. At Ohio, Coach Wren thought differently.

One day, while I was in a slump, Coach Wren suggested I turned around to my natural side for a while. "Just see what happens," he told me.

In my first at-bat from the right side, I hit a long home run against a right-handed pitcher. The experiment worked. I made the all-conference team that year, and All-America the following two seasons. Suddenly, I was on a lot of scouts' lists.

I went off to college as an utter unknown, and I left as a second-round pick of the Philadelphia Phillies. Not too shabby for a walk-on.

Scout: Tony Lucadello

- General Manager: Kansas City Royals 1981–1990
- President and General Manager: Atlanta Braves 1990–2007
- His teams have won their division fifteen times
- World Series Champion: 1985, 1995

JOHN SCHUERHOLZ———•

I know I'm forever a direct reflection of that day.

When I was starting out as a general manager with the Kansas City Royals, I made a trade that was the biggest of my career to that point.

I acquired a dominant, veteran pitcher, knowing that his talent and leadership were exactly what we needed to take our club to the next level.

Sadly, after the trade, I learned he was heavily involved in drugs. And, as the FBI later determined, he was not only using drugs, but he also was distributing them. Unfortunately, the drugs soon showed up in our clubhouse. I was devastated.

Bringing this person into our clubhouse caused so much harm to our club. I felt responsible, but I knew I had to be a leader.

I communicated to everyone in a very direct manner, and I didn't hide from what had happened. I confronted the situation and was honest with reporters, the team, our staff, and our fans. I did not make any excuses and took full responsibility.

During this time, team owner Ewing Kauffman called and asked me to come meet him in his office at Marion Laboratories. Even as the GM, I had never been called to visit him there before.

When I sat down in front of his desk, Mr. Kauffman had his back to his desk. He swiveled around and looked at me with his steady blue eyes, and he pointed his finger at me and said something I'll never forget: "John, we named you GM because we have supreme confidence in you. We don't want you to change because of the circumstances of this deal. We have total confidence in you and know we will all get stronger as a result of this." I could have jumped across the desk to hug him, although thankfully I resisted. But imagine being a young man having these words spoken to you.

He had faith in me at a time when other team owners would have asked for the keys to the franchise back. It taught me faith. It taught me integrity. It taught me strength. It taught me management.

It was a profound and meaningful experience at a time when I had made a huge mistake. I've used this lesson in my own life, time and time again, because it is a great reminder that good people sometimes make bad decisions. It's a reminder that how you treat people is important. It's about honesty and uncompromising integrity.

You have to face mistakes you've made. You have to constantly show your staff or your teammates how much you care about them and look for ways to restore their confidence and uplift them.

I know I'm forever a direct reflection of that day.

- AVG .295 • Home Runs 407 • RBIs 1,333
- Brooklyn Dodgers 1947–1957, Los Angeles Dodgers 1958–1962, New York Mets 1963, San Francisco Giants 1964
- All-Star: 1950–1956, 1963
- Major League Player of the Year: 1955
- Los Angeles Dodgers career leader in Home Runs (389), RBIs (1,271) and Extra-Base Hits (814)
- Elected to the National Baseball Hall of Fame: 1980

D U K E S N I D E R

You have to love what you do and surround yourself with
people whom you admire and who care about you.

One of the pinnacle moments of my baseball career was in the 1959 World Series against the Chicago White Sox. I came up to bat against Early Winn and hit a home run to win the World Series.

While the whole world watched and my teammates and Dodger fans celebrated, that moment, and my Hall of Fame career, would not have been possible if it were not for a day a little more than a decade before then.

During my first invitation to the Brooklyn Dodgers spring training in Vero Beach, Florida, in 1948, I was a twenty-one-year-old on the brink of turning my childhood dream of playing big league ball into reality. It was this goal that was driving my every waking moment.

Every moment of my life up until this point had prepared me for this opportunity, and I was excited and confident to prove myself and earn a spot on the big league club.

Upon arriving, I met with Dodgers president Branch Rickey.

Branch said to me, "Duke, you are a swinger, but you are not a hitter. You do not know your own strike zone, and you swing at everything. You'll never make it at this level unless you learn to improve on your weaknesses right now before you develop bad habits and miss your opportunity."

Though my desire to make it to the next level was greater than own youthful stubbornness, apparently so was my strike zone. Branch's critique of my hitting could have been very difficult for me to hear because the press was saying that I had a swing like Joe DiMaggio and that I was going to be a big part of the future of the Dodgers. It is very easy to start believing in what is being said about you and how you feel about yourself versus what is truly the reality.

Since about the fourth grade, my skills on the baseball field were so superior that I did not even know what a slump was until I started playing pro ball. Like many young ballplayers, I worked on what I was great at because it was easier, and when I was a kid, I did not always have the discipline to work and overcome my weaknesses. All I knew until then was that I wanted to be a big league ballplayer and that I could depend on my abilities and talents to be a great player. That alone had gotten me to this point, so I never even thought it would be any different at the major league level.

After the talk with Branch, I quickly realized that in order to know the game and to play it well, you have to know yourself and your capabilities and, most importantly, ask for help and accept help when someone cares enough about you to give it to you.

It is a very difficult lesson to realize you are doing something wrong in any field, and correcting your flaws is a challenge that anyone must overcome. And the sooner you can learn this lesson, the longer you will be able to sustain a greater level of success.

The key is to have the confidence to put your ego aside, recognize your flaws, and have a greater desire to succeed over all obstacles. I wasn't always the easiest guy to get along with because I was so hard on myself, but my desire to succeed always surpassed my own stubbornness.

I also recognized that Branch wanted me to succeed as badly as I did, so that made it much easier for me to listen to him.

There were many people who were giving me advice at this time, but you have to be selective of whom you take advice from. It is so important to take advice from people who care about you and understand and share your goals. This was the road to for me to reach my potential. It was at this moment that I realized that becoming a big league ballplayer was no longer just my goal, but now it was the Dodgers' goal as well.

That day, Branch, along with coach George Sisler, put me in a batting cage. It was the same type of batting cage I had been in a thousand times as a kid with a pitcher, catcher, and an umpire. Only this time, one essential item was missing.

My bat.

Branch and George put me in the cage without my bat. They forced me to go through my normal stance without holding a bat. I was instructed to stride toward the ball and call out the type of pitch and where it landed in the catcher's mitt. We did this exercise repeatedly for about a week to reinforce where my strike zone was and where it wasn't until I got it right.

The next week they let me have my bat, but I was only thrown slow curves, and I was required to hit every pitch to the shortstop side of second base.

I thought initially that this drill was simply teaching me to wait for the ball because I was soon hitting four hundred-foot home runs to left field. Then, I realized that the goal was to make me a more complete hitter. I was becoming a hitter because Branch and George's advice allowed me to identify what I could do and couldn't do.

I was too young to realize it at the time, but the lessons learned in those few weeks were the keys to my success at the plate, and it helped me to understand that you have to be open to taking advice and learning from it at all points of your career.

Whether you are a doctor, an accountant, or a ballplayer, you have to love what you do and surround yourself with people you admire and that care about you. Branch was an astute baseball mind, and we all knew he had the ability to look into the future and see our potential and limitations as players who controlled our destinies.

During those weeks in 1948, I felt myself improving, but for the first time it helped me to look around and compare my complete skills with my teammates' abilities, and even though I wanted to be a big league ballplayer more than anything, I realized I wasn't ready.

I spoke with Branch and shared with him my realization, and I felt I needed to go back to the minor leagues and hone my skills to work on my weaknesses so that when I did reach the majors that it would be permanently.

That drill in the cage further helped me to understand a lesson that stayed with me throughout my career. You always need to keep working, and you should always find someone who can help you with what you don't know, because more than likely you don't realize what help you need when you need it most.

Later in the summer of 1948, I was playing for the minor league club in Montreal, and each game was a lesson for me back to those days in Vero Beach in the cages of discipline, consistency, and patience.

Branch came to watch a game in the middle of the summer. That night, I hit two home runs, and Branch came over to me in the locker room and said, "Nice game."

I was so excited to see him and asked him eagerly, "Do you think it was enough to take me back?"

What Branch said to me next were the words I had dreamed of since I was a little boy.

"Pack your bags, Duke. You're on the plane out tonight because you are the starting center fielder tomorrow for the Brooklyn Dodgers."

The next day I started for the Dodgers and never looked back— except to remember the lessons I learned those days in the cage with Branch and George .

While I never repeated the cage drill physically after I made it to the big leagues, I did repeat it mentally every time I stepped in the batter's box. My teammates were a big part of my remembrance, and I learned to depend on them to help me identify my weaknesses throughout my career.

Whether it was Don Drysdale or Ralph Branca reminding me to wait on pitches before I left the dugout, or Jackie Robinson barking out advice from the on-deck circle, I was always a better hitter with someone to help me, and that day helped me to always be open to advice every day of my career.

Looking back, I realize that was what reaching my potential was all about.

My potential to hit the home run in the 1959 World Series and to reach the Hall of Fame would have never been possible had I not received the advice that day in Spring Training and been open to advice and worked at it for all those years.

Scouts: Tom Downey and Clyde Sukeforth

- AVG .279 • Home Runs 292 • RBIs 1,466 • Hits 2,716
- Houston Colt .45's/Astros 1963–1968, Montreal Expos 1969–1971 and 1979, New York Mets 1972–1975 and 1981–1985, Detroit Tigers 1976–1979, Texas Rangers 1980
- Led National League in doubles: 1967
- All-Star: 1967–1971, 1976

R U S T Y   S T A U B ————————•

Ted told me to find people I respect and listen intently to
their advice, and it will open the door to my dreams.

In 1961, when I was a senior on the baseball team at Jesuit High School in New Orleans, we won the championship. The title game was when I met my baseball hero for the first time.

Ted Williams attended the game, and he signed my graduation book. I can remember it like it just happened five minutes ago. He signed it, "To a future big leaguer if I've ever seen one, Ted Williams."

We talked for a few minutes about hitting and hand adjustments. I just tried to soak in as much as my teenage self could handle. Ted told me to find people I could respect and listen intently to their advice. He said it would open the door to my dreams.

A lot of the newspapers had written about me already, but these words were better than any front-page article because they came from my hero. They were powerful words to hear from anyone, but this was Ted Williams. I took his words to heart and sought out people I respected.

One of those people was my first professional hitting coach, Dave Philley, who told me to choke up about two finger widths on the bat. This, he said, would help me with bat control without limiting any of my power. It wasn't mind-boggling advice, but it was simple advice from someone I respected.

It would be another six years before I saw Ted again. By then, I was a member of the 1967 Houston Astros. Ted came to the stadium to throw out the first pitch at one of our games as part of a promotional tour. After he threw the first pitch, he returned to our dugout and sat with us.

In the first inning, Gaylord Perry threw me a fastball over the plate, and I hit a single. I felt pretty good about it, but when I came to the dugout, Ted said, "Nice hitting, but you'll never see that pitch again." I had studied the Giants scouting report very closely and knew their tendencies, so I responded confidently, "I know he'll throw that same first pitch fastball to me, and I'm going to line it for a double next time."

Ted just sat there and did not say anything. I'm not sure anyone has ever spoken to him that way. I was a little surprised by my response myself.

Luckily for me, a great scouting report was on my side that night.

For my next at-bat, I stepped up to the plate, choked up like Dave had taught me, and got another first pitch fastball from Gaylord. Sure enough, I laced it for a line-drive double.

A few batters later, I scored. I was so excited; I raced into the dugout as if I were being chased. Ted was still sitting there. He smiled at me and simply said, "Kid, you're gonna be OK."

I never felt better in my entire life.

Scouts: Earl Harris, Paul Richards, and Connie Ryan

- Rockford Peaches, 1945–1946, Kenosha Comets 1947, Peoria Redwings 1947, South Bend Blue Sox 1948–1950
- Played second base, third base, and utility outfield
- Considered one of the best defensive third basemen in the league
- Won the 1945 Championship with the Rockford Peaches

HELEN
FILARSKI-STEFFES——•

I decided early on that I would do in life only what I loved to do, and nothing was going to get in my way.

I was a teenager in the 1940s, and like everyone else in my neighborhood, I loved baseball. Baseball is what we did in our neighborhood. This might seem like a very common activity at the time, but the only difference was I was a girl.

And many assumed that girls should not play baseball. I did not care about what I supposed to do or listen to people tell me what I could not do. I decided early on in life that I would do only what I loved to do, and nothing was going to get in my way.

That's what dreams are all about in my mind: doing what I love, not what anyone else wants me to do. Why take the time to dream if I couldn't try to make it become a reality?

While it seemed at the time that my love of baseball would be a hobby, I never imagined that I would get the chance, especially as a girl, to get paid to play.

I had heard about a girls' professional league that had started two years earlier, but it did not even seem like a reality for me, even with my ambitious dreams. When I heard of a tryout near my home in Detroit in 1945, I went. I did well enough that I was invited to go to Spring Training in Havana, Cuba, and I earned a roster spot on one of the teams in the All-American Girls Professional Baseball League.

This was incredible to me, but the timing was difficult because I was only fourteen years old at the time. My parents tried to talk me into waiting so I could be a little older, but I had a fire in my belly. Nothing was going to stop me. I knew there was a small window of opportunity because of World War II, and I pushed them into letting me follow my dreams.

They eventually did.

I boarded the flight to Havana and played six seasons for the Rockford Peaches, Kenosha Comets, Peoria Redwings, and South Bend Blue Sox. It was the best decision I ever made because I listened to my heart and had the courage and faith to put that desire in my heart into action

Looking back, I understand more clearly that I achieved my dream because I wasn't afraid. For me, it required taking some chances.

I did not let the obstacle of my parents, my gender, or my age get in the way of recognizing and seizing an opportunity not just to pursue but to live a dream. This was a powerful lesson that guided me for the rest of my life. I never listened to anyone tell me I could not do anything. It is a motto that was the foundation of a life less ordinary for me, and I am so very proud my children and grandchildren have adopted it in their own lives.

- ERA 2.83 • Saves 300
- Chicago Cubs 1976–1980, St. Louis Cardinals 1981–1984, Atlanta Braves 1985–1986, 1988
- All-Star: 1977–1981, 1984
- Cy Young Award: 1979
- Led the league in saves: 1979–1984
- World Series Champion: 1982
- Elected to the National Baseball Hall of Fame: 2006

B R U C E   S U T T E R————————•

Everything changed instantly for me.

In 1972, I signed a five hundred dollar contract with the Chicago Cubs as an undrafted player and went to spring training with hopeful dreams of one day being a big league pitcher.

The politics in those days were simple. If a team invested a high draft pick on a pitcher, they were almost automatically on the path to become a starting pitcher. On the other hand, guys like me that were not drafted were delegated to the bullpen.

In my first few practices, I could sense this separation simply by the way the coaches worked with us. As a relief pitcher, your goal is to have a few out pitches that could get your team out of jams.

During these workouts, my pitching coaches tried to teach me a slider in hopes it would become my out pitch. While trying to learn the proper arm motion, I heard a very loud pop. I actually think it was loud enough that the entire team heard it.

It was my elbow.

The injury was so bad that the Cubs told me to go home and come back when it had healed.

I went back home and just kind of moped around for months, wondering if my chance had been lost. It was a difficult time for me. I was so young, and I believed in my heart that I was destined to be a pitcher in the big leagues, but I was so worried that my chance had passed when my elbow popped.

Then one day, I decided that instead of worrying about it, I would do something about it.

I did not tell the Cubs, but I went to an orthopedic surgeon in Pennsylvania and had my elbow operated on. By the time I returned to spring training the next year, my elbow had regained its strength, and my arm was at full strength again. I was terrified that the Cubs would consider me damaged goods if they knew I had surgery, so I wore long sleeves every time I pitched to conceal my scars.

One day it was so hot that I had to wear short sleeves. One of our coaches, Fred Martin, saw my scar and asked about it.

I had to tell him about the surgery.

To my great surprise, Fred said he would keep it a secret and insisted on teaching me a new pitch. That pitch was the split-finger fastball; it became my signature "out" pitch.

Everything changed instantly for me.

I couldn't wait to try this new pitch in a game. I was assigned to the Cubs' Class A team, and the ball broke so well that no one had a clue where it was going. It was such great feeling that fueled my confidence and faith in my abilities.

I knew in that very moment that my hopeful dreams of becoming a big league pitcher were becoming a reality.

Scout: Ralph DiLullo

- AVG .261 • Home Runs 21 • RBIs 105
- Milwaukee Braves 1955–1957, Chicago Cubs 1957–1958, Cleveland Indians 1959–1960, Los Angeles Angels 1961–1962
- General Manager: Chicago White Sox 1970–1975, Oakland Athletics 1976, Pittsburgh Pirates 1977–1985, Atlanta Braves 1986–1988
- World Series Champion: 1979

CHUCK TANNER ———————•

Armed with my family's "never quit" philosophy, I did not give up on my dream of reaching the big leagues.

When I was eighteen years old, a scout with the Milwaukee Brewers named Jack Reider signed me, and I was assigned to the minor leagues. I was so excited to be a professional baseball player, but my opportunity to play took longer because not too long after that, I became sick. I was hospitalized and was suffering from bleeding ulcers. I became so sick that I was living on baby food for three months, but I learned a valuable lesson during that time that my father had preached to me repeatedly while growing up: *never quit.*

Equally important to never quitting, he also taught me to have compassion for yourself at all times.

Even though I was in immense physical pain and was very weak, I stayed mentally strong and was determined not to get down on myself or return home until I recovered and started playing baseball again.

How could I do anything else?

You see, for my father and my mother, the notion of never quitting was more than words to them; it was their way of life, and their example was ingrained in me. My father was a mill worker, and he would live in a boarding house for five days during the week while working endless tough hours at the mill before returning to his family on the weekends.

He never gave up, and faced with this obstacle of a health injury, I believed neither would I.

I believed in these words because my parents showed it to me with their actions all those years, but the time I spent with the bleeding ulcers proved it to me for myself. This helped me to continually to reach and exceed my dreams not only in this situation but in countless other moments when quitting might have seemed the right thing to do.

Like every minor league ballplayer, my goal was to reach the next level and play in the major leagues. Even though I hit above .300 for eight years in the minor leagues, I never got the chance to play in the big leagues.

But armed with my family's never quit philosophy, I did not give up on my dream of reaching the big leagues.

I realized at this moment I would not have a long career as a ballplayer, so using the same code of never quitting when I had my health problems as a teenager, I turned my focus to reaching the major leagues as a manager.

I ended up having a wonderful career as manager of the Chicago White Sox, Atlanta Braves and even won a World Series as manager of the Pittsburgh Pirates, and none of these incredible life experiences would have been possible without understanding what it takes to be successful and sustain it over time.

The first thing you have to have in order to be successful in anything, beyond any talent you may posses, is the determination to never quit. It's the most important attitude you can have, and I've applied it to every area of my life and relentlessly encouraged all of my players to use this attitude in their own careers.

People that never quit will overcome adversity when things are not going so well because they are not afraid to fail, because if they do, they know they will just work harder. That is the difference right there to becoming successful. You need to go through this lesson if you are going to succeed on the baseball diamond or on any other field you enter.

Scout: Jack Reider

- AVG .295 • Home Runs 184 • Hits 1,826
- Houston Astros 1966–1979, Boston Red Sox 1979, New York Yankees 1980–1982, Atlanta Braves 1982–1984
- Became the first African American general manager in the major leagues with the Houston Astros in 1993
- All-Star: 1973, 1975
- General Manager: New York Yankees 1995–1998
- World Series Champion: 1996

BOB WATSON——————.

The only person that can make you feel intimidated is
yourself.

It was the early 1960s, and I was a teenager growing up in South Central Los Angeles. At that time, South Central LA was a baseball haven, and all I thought about was baseball.

I played on several teams, and my grandmother used to drive me from team to team in her Plymouth station wagon, and I would change uniforms in her car on the way to the park.

One of the teams I played on was the Pittsburgh Pirates rookie team that was managed by former Negro League Baseball pitcher Chet Brewer. Everyone in the neighborhood wanted to be on this team because of the talent we had. I was the catcher on the team that also included Paul Blair, Willie Crawford, Doc Ellis, Leon McFadden, Charlie Murray, Dave Nelson, Reggie Smith, Roy White, and Don Wilson.

Just about everybody on that team went on to play professional baseball, and we were all just teenagers. It was such a great time in my life.

Chet was the guy who taught us everything about baseball and about life. He was especially good to me because I was a catcher, and he had pitched in the Negro Leagues. He would give me little tidbits on how to read pitchers and when to communicate with pitchers on the mound.

These little things amounted to big lessons that helped me tremendously along the way to the big leagues.

When I was drafted by the Houston Colt .45's, I could still hear Chet's voice.

"Do this. Do that."

His lessons were a big part of me and were a big reason I was now a professional baseball player.

One of those lessons really helped me when I reached the big leagues.

Chet told me to never to be intimidated by a pitcher or anyone in life.

"The only person that can make you feel intimidated is yourself—not a pitcher," Chet said to me repeatedly.

I was 6'10" and nicknamed the "Bull", so I was used to intimidating the pitchers. That is, until I reached the big leagues.

I remember thinking back to Chet's advice when I stepped into the plate against Los Angeles Dodgers pitcher Don Drysdale.

I did not ever do very well against Drysdale, but I can honestly say that he never intimidated me, and that lesson from Chet is one of the many he taught me that I think of still to this day.

Scout: Karl Kuehl

- Joined the league at age fourteen
- South Bend Blue Sox 1947, Kenosha Comets 1948–1951, Fort Wayne Daisies 1952–1953
- Won two pennants with the Fort Wayne Daisies
- Earned her doctorate from the University of Southern Mississippi
- Served as president of the AAGPBL

DOLLY BRUMFIELD-WHITE ———•

We drive our dreams, but you need angels to come into your life who help you along the way.

When I stop and think about it, one thing is very true in all of our lives: none of us gets to do what we want to do in life on our own.

We drive our dreams, but you need angels to come into your life who help you along the way. My opportunity as a woman to play professional baseball for the All-American Girls Professional Baseball League was no different.

Well, except maybe that I had the benefit of not just one but three angels who had an impact on my baseball career. One got me into the league. One gave me the gift of their time, and the final one taught me the game.

Grady Branch was a neighbor of ours in Mobile, Alabama, and he would spend his afternoons playing pitch and catch with me after work. I don't remember my own dad playing catch with me, but I remember spending hours with Mr. Branch.

He gave me the most precious gift you can give a child: time. He used that time to teach me baseball skills, and I also learned to appreciate the gift of time. He's the first person that made a difference. Mr. Branch talked to me about passions in life, and it ignited a life of following my heart. He shared with me his passion for baseball, and it became my passion. There's a unique power in spending time with someone when they are young, and I was the benefactor of Mr. Branch's kindness.

With the love of baseball ingrained in my heart, I knew I wanted to be a baseball player.

Because of the circumstances of World War II, a new women's baseball league was formed, and I made the South Bend Blue Sox. I was only fourteen years old and the youngest girl on the team, and that's when I met my second angel: Chet Grant. Chet was our manager, and before coaching this team, he was a quarterback at Notre Dame on the team that Knute Rockne starred on.

We would have practice, and Chet knew how young I was, but he gave me the gift of his time. He would spend extra moments with me after practice and invited me to sit on the bench with him so I could ask questions and learn from him.

In 1948, the league expanded, and Chet switched teams. He became the manager of the Kenosha club, and he drafted me in the expansion draft. He spent even more time working with me and teaching me. My earlier realization that this gift of time is the most precious gift you can give someone was once again proven true as I gained confidence and playing time as a result of Chet's wisdom.

It was during my pro career that I met my third angel: Fred McCaughan. Fred was the father of one of my teammates in Kenosha. Fred worked at the local Studebaker plant. As much as Chet would push me as a ballplayer, Fred stayed on me repeatedly to get my education. At the time it was not customary for a girl to go to college.

But then again, girls were not supposed to play professional baseball either, right?

In fact, my own father told me that girls don't go to college, but all of these influences from the outside shaped my thinking. I was destined for a different life—both on and off the baseball diamond.

Not only did I follow Fred's urging and get a college degree, but I spent my post-baseball career as an educator. And whether I was on the baseball diamond or in the classroom, the best lesson I learned from the people that shaped my passions to play baseball and help people was how much they cared for me and gave me the most precious gift of all: time.

- AVG .290 • Home Runs 426 • Hits 2,711
- Chicago Cubs 1959–1974, Oakland Athletics 1975–1976
- National League Rookie of the Year: 1961
- All-Star: 1962, 1964–1965, 1968, 1972–1973
- The Sporting News Player of the Year: 1972
- Elected to the National Baseball Hall of Fame: 1987

BILLY WILLIAMS———•

Good. Better. Best. Never rest until the good is better, and
the better is best.

I imagined my destiny changed the moment I put on the Chicago Cubs uniform for the first time and made my major league debut.

That was the realization of a dream and hard work, and I have several pivotal moments in my life that made this dream moment a reality.

The best moments in life, I believe, are those that are grounded in truths. For me, the truest moment of my life happened to me while I was in grade school. During an in-school assembly, our principal, Miss Lillie Dixon, said, "Good. Better. Best. Never rest until the good is better and the better is best."

I didn't realize it at the time, but those words had a profound impact on how I approached everything in life. Miss Lillie created a pattern of optimism, hard work, and mentorship that established a foundation of dreams for me in baseball that carried me through my childhood and into high school.

When I was close to finishing high school, I was playing for the Mobile Black Bears. We had a good team that played throughout the South. Tommie Aaron was on our team. He was our star player, and all the scouts came to see him.

Or so I thought.

After a game one afternoon, a teammate of mine said there was a scout in the stands from the Cubs there to see me.

Even though he told me this, I still went about my business and presumed that he was there for Tommie. I continued to play, and eventually I learned that the scout's name was Ivy Griffin. I also realized that maybe he was, in fact, looking at me.

Before I could sign, I had to wait until I got my high school diploma, but Ivy started talking to my dad about playing with the Cubs. Within a few days after graduation, I signed a contract with Ivy and the Cubs, and I was off to Oklahoma to start my professional career.

Like a lot of young adults entering a man's world, I was very concerned about my future because I didn't really know what I wanted to do. Even though I signed a contract, baseball still seemed like such a far-reaching dream that it was hard to believe that I could make it all the way to the big leagues and stay there.

I really struggled the first few years in the minors—both at home plate and being away from home. Even though I had made it to Class AA ball, I still was not sure I belonged with the guys at the next level. I missed my family, and the social challenges of the time for an African American made it very difficult.

In my frustration, I quit the team.

Thankfully, Cubs coach Buck O'Neil followed me home. I was at a crossroad in my life, but I was too young to realize it. Buck knew it, and he would not let me quit.

Buck reassured me, "Son, you have more to offer the world. Your dream is not over yet. It is only beginning, and you were born to be a baseball player."

Then, we just walked in silence.

Only the conversation continued not in words but in the scenery as we silently walked through the path Buck had chosen for us to walk. He purposely took me through Pritchard Park, a park in my hometown. Everywhere we turned, people were making a big deal out of me. They were saying I was living their dream, and it gave them a strong sense of pride to know we were from the same town.

Buck had taken me to an atmosphere that allowed me to understand his teachings, and it worked. It was at that moment that I realized what an honor it is to have a gift. I can honestly say I never looked back.

Within a few years, I made it to Class AAA and battled future Hall of Famer Carl Yastremzki for the batting title. I won the Rookie of the Year for the Cubs in 1961 and went on to play in 1,117 consecutive games.

As much as any mechanical hitting lesson, Miss Lillie's words and Buck's love carried me to Cooperstown. To compete on a higher level in those days with only sixteen teams, you could not get complacent, and understanding your responsibility to others and always striving for more are the reasons I had success.

Scout: Ivy Griffin

ACKNOWLEDGMENTS———.

Dreams.

Legendary All-American Girls Professional Baseball League star Dolly Brumfield-White shared with me, "We drive our dreams, but you need angels to come into your life that help you along the way."

While I'm blessed to be surrounded by countless angels, there are some I'd like to acknowledge for helping give both this project, and me, wings to soar.

This book isn't possible without the heart and passion of one man: Roland Hemond. Roland, your heart-leadership in baseball over the last half century is a legacy that will shape the future of the game.

Starting Lineup

A book like this requires a team of supporters, and here's my team managed by—who else—my cherished friend Mike Veeck.

1 • Joe Balazs

2 • Sean Brenner

3 • Brad Horn

4 • Jeff Idelson

5 • Josh Kritzler

6 • Paul and Diane Migala

7 • Katie Migala

8 • Ron Seaver

9 • Kristina Skrela

All-Century Team

A few years ago, MasterCard and Major League Baseball ran a promotion to name baseball's All-Century Team. If I may be so bold, I'd like to use this opportunity to recognize my own Century Team of—in Dolly Brumfield-White's words—"angels" that have come into my life, both directly in helping with this project, learning lessons from them and in their boundless love and inspiration for me.

Ray Artigue, Brad Barton, Big Al, Jason Bitsoff, Brooks Boyer, Ken Brenner, Beth Brockert, Tim Brosnan, David Brown, Tommy Byrne, Matt Clay, Paula Clay, Diana Corte, Curious George, Barrett Davie, Mr. & Mrs. William Davis, Dewey, Joe Dumars, Steve Dupee, Bob Dylan, Kristin Endress, Kristen Faron, David Frimml, Tom Garfinkel, Kristen Gengaro, Doris Kearns Goodwin, Mike Gordon, Stedman Graham, Ethan Green, Ryan Gribble, Darrin Gross, Meghann Gunderman, Garry Gupton, Terrie Gupton, Craig Hajduk, Lynn Hajduk, Derrick Hall, John Hammond, Karen Head, Tom Hecht, Suzette Heiman, Jay Hemond, Margo Hemond, Susan Hemond, Kathleen Hessert, Tracy Hodson, Dalton Hunter, Dillon Hunter, Shawn Hunter, Sanaa Julien, Jim Kahler, Rob Katz, Jerry Kavanagh, Jane Kleinberger, Dr. Terri Klemm, David Kritzler, Peggy Kritzler, Amy Latimer, Mark Lemmon, Paul Lettieri, Mrs. Loesch, Molly Lowe, Dr. Ken Mace, A. J. Maestas, Barry Manilow, Kalli Martin, Ed McCaskey, Jamie McKenna, Mark McLatchey, Linda McNabb, Grandpa Emil Migala, Grandma Irene Migala, Nick Migala, Bill Miller, Jim Miller, Marin Milio, Dean Mills, David Mullins, Jim Muno, Jeffrey Moorad, Dr. Michael Mokwa, Grandma Margaret Molinari, Grandpa Tony Molinari, Michael Myers, Erin Nangle, Nancy Nesnidal, Steve Neff, Alicia Nevins, Jeff Ney, Margaret Papas, Andrew Pate, Ryan Peck, Dale Petroskey, Alice Petzold, Ted Philips, Presley, John Poehlman, Ann Quint, Rene Rau, Marianne Riddell, Michelle Robie, Mark Rockefeller, Jill Rusinko, Jennifer Russo, Josh St. John, Rebecca Schmid, Anouk Schneider, Kathy Schwab, Jeff Sedivy, Dianne Shabat, Aunt Genny Smith, Andy Strasberg, David Spain, Don Sullivan, Teresa Tedrow, Dawn Tutt, Mike Tutt, Roger Valdiserri, Libby Veeck, Rebecca Veeck, Tom Whaley, Gary Wheeler, Deborah Wilk, Tim Wiles, Ethan Willis, and Michael Young.

Special thanks also goes to our talented research director—and future baseball star—Zane Hemond. And lastly, to all the wonderfully friendly baristas at Starbucks whose smiles and coffee smoke swirls kept me going while writing the pages of this book.

Beyond the Baselines
This project requires an intuitive business sense, and thankfully we have the best in the business managing this book from day one in Josh Kritzler. In his words, here are a few people he'd like to thank.

"A few years ago my friend Dan allowed me to share in what has become one of the most significant personal and professional journeys of my life. Seeing passion realized on a daily basis through the creation of this book is truly inspiring. I wanted to thank a few people who, like this book, continue to inspire me each and every day. My soon-to-be wife, Natalie, the most wonderful, generous, and caring person I've ever known. David, Peg, Emily, and Abby Kritzler, the greatest support system a person could ask for. The author, for his friendship, creativity, vision, and passion. Woody Levin, who convinced me to take the road less traveled. David Shook, whose life lessons are always with me. To the memory of Elaine Shook, one of the most courageous people I've ever had the privilege of knowing. And to my late Grandpa Sidney Kritzler, the original entrepreneur."
• Josh Kritzler

Breinigsville, PA USA
15 December 2009
229258BV00001B/220/P